Antón Ponce de León

In Search of the Wise ONE

A Sacred Journey

Antón Ponce de León Paiva
(I.A. Uma)

In Search
of the
Wise ONE
A Sacred Journey

Bluestar
Communications
Woodside, California

Translated by Mary Clark, Ph.D.
First published in Spanish in Peru by
Municipality of Cuzco, Plaza Kusipata; Cuzco, Peru under the title
En Busca del Anciano
Copyright © 1994 by Antón Ponce de León Paiva

This translation:

Copyright © 1996 Bluestar Communications
44 Bear Glenn
Woodside, CA 94062
Tel: 800-6-Bluestar

Edited by Goddess Enterprises
Cover Art by Petra Michel

First printing 1996

ISBN: 1-885394-16-0

Ponce de León Paiva, Antón, 1930-
    [En busca del anciano. English]
    In search of the wise one : a sacred journey / Antón Ponce de León
Paiva, I.A. Uma ; [translated by Mary Clark].
        p. cm.
    Includes bibliographic references.
    ISBN 1-885394-16-0
    1. Quechua Indians—Religion. 2. Quechua philosophy.
3. Spiritual life—Andes Religion. 4. Andes Region—Religious life
and customs. I. Uma, I.A., 1930- . II. Title.
F2230.2.K4P6613 1996
299'.883--dc20
                                                  95-26724
                                                        CIP

Printed in USA

Dedication

To You—Father, Grand Architect, and sublime Builder of this beauty called Earth.
It is your pure manifestation, as is all of the Universe.

To Cuzco, sacred city of the Runasimi.

To my dear brothers in the Solar Brotherhood (H.S.I.CH.) in your respective retreats.

To my brother Yosip Ibrahin (José Rosciano), who has now departed.

To Vitko Novi (Vlado Kapetanovic).

To all the musicians and singers of this Incan land, to the groups Metáfora and Arco Iris, to Rina Venero and Marlyn Pacheco, 'Pablucha Venero' and Carlos Alvarez.

To my children and grandchildren. I also have been, and will continue being.

Acknowledgment

The first beat remains in our hearts. Thank you Rolando.
To Gaby and Andreas—our love and special recognition.
To Pinky, Maricarmen, Lula, Araceli, Elvira, Beatriz, and
Antonio for your help and continual love.

To Marie Helen, Mabel, Inty (Rudiger) and Delila—your
labor in Samana Wasi is invaluable and impartial.

To Zoila and Camilo for serving us with your time and
work in Samana Wasi.

To Estela, Beatriz, and Enrique—your cooperation in the
preparation and health of our children in Samana Wasi.

To Ursula, Axel, Marijana, Jaques, Gerd, Peter, and La
Asociación Amigos de la Nueve Era de Acuario [Friends
of the New Age of Aquarius Association], who help us
perseveringly and silently.

To Gloria Luz and Norma for being my 'secretaries'.

To Ana and Eloísa—your love and persistent help.

To Janín, Jorge, Luis, and family.

To Carlos, Pepe, and Wasi for your inestimable friendship.

To Mario and Erwin—you supported the major presenta-
tion of this modest work.

To Teresita—our love and eternal gratitude.

Gratitude

My eternal gratitude remains with Regia. You are all women rolled into one for me—my wife, mother, companion, friend, and sister—for your love, dedication, and tolerance.

To the Honorable Provincial Municipality of Cuzco in the person of its mayor, Dr. Daniel Estrada Pérez—for the Peruvian edition of this book.

Preface

There are extraordinary events that seem exceptional and unreal. They appear fantastic or difficult to accept, but nevertheless *are*. Each day I become increasingly convinced of their existence and influence in our lives.

I have no pretense of authority, nor do I insist that any one accepts these events. This is a statement of what I witnessed—I saw, heard, and lived it. *He* knows the truth of these narrations and their intent.

Antón Ponce de León Paiva, Samana Wasi

Contents

Foreword

Since the appearance of *The Wisdom of the Ancient One*, this has been a long-awaited book. Its author, Antón Ponce de León Paiva, has penetrated the fascinating world of occult knowledge, bringing to light in a delightful narration, simple but wise teachings that have remained unknown for more than five hundred years. That is to say, these teachings are present in our most remote Andean communities, constituting the true cultural resistance to the Occidental presence.

The novelesque style permits the author to combine fiction with his need to share a message of great spiritual beauty. This message—now in force and quite contemporary—redeems the most authentic cultural Andean roots.

Whoever read the first book (in one of its ten editions translated in seven languages) will find that this sequel presents two levels: A new way of viewing life will emerge from the ideas of Andean spirituality, and the words of Amaru also introduce new teachings that, being part of the universal wisdom, reveal a viewpoint and perception from our culture.

Reading this book will arouse reflections in each of us. We have all anxiously awaited some new seeds of change such as these; they not only urge us to evolve as individuals but to facilitate change in our society.

Antón Ponce de León Paiva is not merely a writer. He is not merely a good interpreter of the mysteries of the universal and Andean spirituality. He is a man whose life is a persistent practice, since Samana Wasi has become a beautiful reality—the mission that Nina Soncco placed upon Ponce.

Cuzco, June 1994
Carlos Milla Vidal

11

Prologue

I asked Nina Soncco[1] for his support to verify the telling of his story and of mine—this would facilitate the acceptance of this book. He made it known, in no uncertain terms, that he would not do this, that vanity is dangerous. He stated that this story would be accepted by all who are humble and pure of heart; skeptics and the proud would denounce and criticize it. In spite of his admonition, I will continue—I will write this. There is not a moment to waste. I will write present it to the mercy of each person's honesty.

The events I am about to narrate happened seven years after my return from Village A.[2] The past has no greater importance. Its validity is eternal, as is all truth. This is so now more than ever in the difficult circumstance of living.

A stubborn man persists in believing that he is what he perceives himself to be, rather than what he is in reality. He is the cause of all the disastrous ways in which he lives. His personality becomes intellectualized, vain, and confused by many concepts. His identity ought to reflect the real person—unfortunately, it does not. Knowledge and experience are synonymous for him; esoterically they are not. Finally, he mistakes the path and searches for God where he can never find Him.

We must reinstate the archetypal standard to adjust our lives properly and sincerely. I learned this during many additional visits to *Ccusilluchayoc* (The Place of the Monkeys), which is still known by that name.

Ccusilluchayoc is situated a few miles north by northeast of Cuzco. This is a very important archeological cluster located in the Archeological Park of Sacsaywamán. It conceals the entrance to another dimension. A puma sculpted in stone watches as its guardian. Monkeys have been carved in bas-relief on a large block of granite; some look to the north and

13

others to the south. A zigzagging serpent—also in bas-relief—meanders up a column of rock. What were the Ancient Ones saying through these symbols? Beyond the portal I found recessed and raised stone carvings of circles and ellipses of different sizes. No doubt these symbolize many esoteric enigmas. There they lie in ruins of decay and vandalism—abandoned. What anguish! It is an even greater offense to know that people who feel committed to spiritualism will also plunder these sacred grounds; they carry away stones to use as amulets. The structure has fallen into complete ruin by the ravages of man and the passage of time.

Once while I was puzzling over the occult significance behind these silent sculptures, I felt the presence of someone behind me. The sun shone directly over my shoulders. It was ten o'clock on a day near the June winter solstice. I was looking westward and contemplating these massive, imposing stone sculptures with admiration and respect. Again I felt the strange sensation that someone was following me. I could not tolerate it any more. I whirled around to see who had arrived so silently.

Surprise! A cold sweat broke out all over my back. Tremendous surprise! He was here! He seemed to be transparent. Incredible! I could see through him to the rocks behind. However, at the same time he seemed so physical that I had the desire to embrace him. Amaru Cusiyupanqui—the Gray-Haired One[3]! This was the father of Chaska whom I met in Village A. He was an intimate friend of the dear and ever remembered teacher *Nina Soncco*. He was here! Close behind me—six to nine feet away, no more— he looked at me very sweetly. I felt afraid; his apparition was unsettling. Seeing those rocks through his body shook me greatly; I was sweating. I wanted to approach, but I could not walk.

He raised his arms in a gesture for me to stay put. He smiled reassuringly and said, "Don't be afraid."

His lips did not move, but I heard him! His voice resonated within me. He seemed very real! He was completely trans-

14

parent. I could see through him to the grassy ground. The sun was now almost at its zenith.

"I have come to see you because we have to talk about some things that are very important at this time," he continued to speak in that inner way, without moving his lips.

He had not aged. His long, frosty hair was as I remembered—a little thinner perhaps. He stood tall, youthful, and erect. He seemed hardly more than fifty years old; chronologically he must have been at least eighty. He smiled again. The expression on my face must have been amusing.

Perhaps he guessed my thoughts—but was he *guessing?* He *knew* my thoughts. He was the one chosen by Nina Soncco to be his successor!

"I am, and yet I am not.

"You are not mistaken," he said. "This place is very special. Thousands of years ago, men had forgotten their past. They reverted to being very primitive. Then, handsome men in 'metal birds' arrived from those mountains." He motioned to the west. "They landed here, in this very place. They were the same as we but more evolved."

"Lemurians?" I wondered.

"They tried to teach science and art to the natives. They cohabited and interbred with the primitives. They are our ancestors; we are the very remote descendants of these men. The future of this hybrid race is our past. The people of Ccusilluchayoc did not know how to profit from the teachings of these ancestors. The beautiful society that we know and all of these wonders that today's world admires were built later."

I did not understand him at all. I thought, here lie the ancient dreams of our past. What happened to the Inca? What of their supposed socially and spiritually superior state?

The Inca did not construct these megalithic walls that we love so much. A very ancient and wise culture had raised these cyclopean works. When had this actually happened? Did the Inca inherit the final remainder of this civilization—

15

now divided and degenerated—and absorb it for their own empire? This ancient culture surely maintained a relationship with the builders of the giant sculptures on Easter Island. On that site are walls very similar to those at the sanctuary of Sacsaywamán (in the city of Cuzco) and Tiahuanacu (near La Paz, Bolivia).

His very strong 'voice' awoke me from my hypnotic reverie. "The walls of this island, which you are thinking about, were copied from ours."

"I will not be able to answer all of your questions—not right now." He continued his explanation.

"After a very long time—hundreds or thousands of years—the few that remained departed in their metal birds. They went in the direction of those mountains to the north and disappeared. Some of their remains will be discovered soon. Perhaps then, scientists may accept that our origin is cosmic.

"Man is but briefly on this earth. Our home is beyond the stars. We are not from this planet, our birthplace; a different planet is our origin. Afterwards—finally reaching their goals—our brothers appeared at the Sacred Lake—Lake Titicaca—with the same intentions.

"Go to Samana Wasi[4] tomorrow. There we will meet again."

Of course, (without taking into account his last words) he had referred to the legend of Manco Capac and Mama Ocllo, teachers of Lake Titicaca. A certain Beltrán García (mentioned in *Land Without Time* by Peter Kolosimo) was reputedly a descendant of Garcilaso de la Vega the Inca. García wrote:

"In the Tertiary (geological era following the Mesozoic) almost five million years ago, when no human being existed on our planet, populated only by fantastic animals, a resplendent spaceship (as if made of gold) came to land on the Island of the Sun (Lake Titicaca). From that spaceship disembarked a woman. Her body from the feet to the breasts resembled the bodies of our women. However her head had a

16

conical shape, huge ears, and her hands were webbed with four fingers."

I also remembered that someone aptly said, "Perhaps Túpac Amaru is the last *orejón* (the one with big ears) of Perú with rights to the Tiana…"

In 1638, Fernando Montesinos mentioned the *chinkanas* (tunnels) in *Ancient Historical Political Memories of Perú*: "Tiahuanacu and Cuzco are joined by a gigantic subterranean road. The Inca do not remember who built it. No one knows about the inhabitants of Tiahuanacu, either. They say that the people who built it retired afterwards to the interior of the Amazon jungle…"

It is possible. Our history is like a tome; it contains everything. However it could be—it could be! I mused again on the lithic monkeys designed in bas-relief.

"What did they signify?" I asked Amaru Cusiyupanqui.

Not hearing his 'voice', I turned to see the reason for his silence. He was no longer there; he had vanished! I lingered a few more minutes and stared at the place where he had appeared. The sun had passed its meridian. It could have been a dream—or was it reality? Perhaps I was dreaming.

Well, tomorrow I would have an answer.

The First Day

I arrived early. Despite the winter, I was breathing air that was warmer in every way than the valley Sacsaywamán. This was my home—the farmhouse of my parents and the future site of Samana Wasi. I felt impatient and doubtful; I left the house and walked toward Samana Wasi. Amaru Cusiyupanqui[1] was sitting on a rock in the stream. Feeling very emotional, I approached him. He rose and I greeted him (as they had shown me in Village A). I embraced him with all of my love.

It had been seven years! I had nearly forgotten. What emotion I was feeling—he was part of my life and my family. There was a lump in my throat; I could not speak. As I gripped his hand and embraced him, I felt the warmth of his heart. He was wearing a maroon poncho with green, vertical rays. It triggered in me fond memories and transported me to another time. With all the beauty of many suns (illuminating more than the sun of that cold morning in June) fleeting images of my beloved friends Amaru Yupanqui Puma, Nina Soncco & his wife, Chaska, Pumaccawa, and the others passed before me. I saw the entire village of my yearning; I longed more than once to return to it but could not because of my vow of word and honor. This surprising vision left me mute; I hoped that it was real.

"Events and doubts always surprise you, even when you have an abundance of proof," he said to me. I noted with relief that his lips moved normally—my proof that he was not a vision.

"I will help you clarify some of what you saw. Sit down," he said. "Our Master Illac Uma Nina Soncco is gone. I, his humble servant, have succeeded him. I now try to follow his teachings and share them with those who are truly deserving. This responsibility worries me a great deal, as I do not have his wisdom and I frequently make mistakes."

"Master Amaru," I interrupted him. "Your modesty and humility are virtues of the Great Ones. Our dear Nina Soncco did not make a mistake. He knew what you had done and therefore he knew you very well. He could not have left our Brotherhood in better hands."

He ignored my remark and continued: "Nina Soncco passed on the seventh full moon after your leaving. As of last summer, seven years have passed since your visit."

I was not keeping track of time and events so precisely. I could not remember exactly how much time had elapsed since my return from the village. It seemed only yesterday.

"When the beloved Illac Uma Amaru Yupanqui Puma departed, the hut where he lived became completely illuminated. It seemed as bright as daylight to those of us who 'saw'. Do you remember?"

"Yes, Master," I replied.

"You were still a little boy then."

"I believe that you too were no more than fifteen years old yourself," I thought.

"I repeat, you were still a little boy but with abilities ahead of others. You were awake during the night before your return home. You watched the light and the other phenomena. We knew your future would be difficult with a great deal of pain, including physical distress. Yes, your life was hard. You have suffered—true?"

"Yes, I suffered a great deal," I responded. I was now feeling removed, very far away.

"This is as it should be." He said. "Happiness and pain are like day and night. We have to accept them and we have to live them. In the same way when our beloved Master Nina Soncco left, the hut also transformed itself into a bell of light. Again we saw another 'star' moving above us in the sky over the village. Many older very special brothers passed to the dimension of the Inti. The

20

pachamama became a burden for his body and he left it for another mission to other places."

He paused and as if returning to this reality said, "Do you remember Quispinga?"

"I cannot place him. I am not sure who he is."

"This is one of your faults that needs to be corrected," he said in a low voice as if to avoid my hearing, but I did hear it. "The first day that you were in the village, you had your first interview with the Illac Uma Nina Soncco. Later in the afternoon, you went to the field where various older men were working. There you conversed with some youths who were taking a short rest, drinking chicha and joking. One of them commented to you that his father had known your father, and he had received the teachings from Nina Soncco with some other fellows."

"Of course. Now I remember. Juan—Juan Quispinga. It is possible that I also knew him when I was very little."

"Yes, that is the man. He married Chaska, and they have three sons. They are happy, and I love my grandchildren very much. Well, it is just an expression, nothing more; I love everything and everyone. Surely, you have already learned this.

"It is very important to love and to love oneself. Man forgot to love himself, and because of this he does not respect himself. How then can he love others? How terrible not to love! It is because of this that we see so many embittered faces on people who walk the earth. They do not know how to enjoy life. Nobody told them—or they have forgotten—that they came here to be happy, in spite of everything. Inti, God, is very just. He did not create us to be unhappy. On the contrary, everything manifested is perfect. The unhappiness that we have created by our actions is the consequence of our attitudes. This is all part of the law of causation, of karma. This is the law. You know it as many people do; they are content to stagnate—knowing the principle without making it their own wisdom. It is not their experience. Our master, Nina Soncco, also spoke to you about this and other laws.

21

These are always in effect. We abide by negative or positive consequences when we fail them or fulfill them. It is very simple and easy."

"It may be easy and simple for you, but not for us." I said.

"It is easy for he who grasps consciousness of reality and applies these laws. It is a question of fulfilling them, nothing more. Does it cost you to work well? To serve correctly? The cosmic rules merely require the following: Work without injuring others. Do not exploit your brother. Be fair in your proceedings. Love."

How right he was, but how difficult it seemed to me.

"All religions teach the correct ways to work and to love others. Yet the majority of faithful churchgoers do not love. Consequently, they do not do good works. In order to save themselves, they have hoped, down the centuries, that someone might come or might return to help them. Did the sacrifice of these Special Beings serve any purpose? Their apparent followers might have answered such a question. It is very common to hope that someone powerful may come or may return to solve humanity's problems. The probability is that no one will come."

"And the Christ, Master?" I asked.

"They erroneously interpret the Return. This will not come about as many people believe or hope. The Return will be given to each one, as he becomes aware of His True Being, that is Him."

"Master," I said to him, "Jesus counseled '*Search for perfection and more will be given unto you.*' The answer to all is within each one of us. There is where we dwell."

"Inti made us conscious of our immortality," said Amaru. "Noccan Cani, the *I Am*, is the seed of immortality. Then, we will understand what life is. We will know what it means to die in order to live and to be truly one and the same. Death is the dream that precedes the true life. How much fear there is of physical death! We really ought to fear our non-accomplishments. That is to say, when you die, cry over the death of what you left unfulfilled. You will have another opportunity to pay your debts according to karma and reincarnation. The permanence in which you believe does not have permanence.

"Stop being the sun that is born in the west—the sepulcher of sun. Be the messenger of the dawn. Many people walk in darkness. Even worse—bad karma—is when they allow others to fall into it. May we not add more obscurity to the obscurity of man. Inti-God is Light. In Him there are no shadows. If we say that we are with Him but walk in darkness, we are shameless liars. It is time to be truthful with ourselves. Spiritual attitudes must be carried through to practice. Only in this way will we progress. The destiny of man is to find himself. Let us love Inti who is our father. He is the fountain of the Great Energy. He is the primordial cause of everything that exists—manifest and unmanifest—as Absolute Truth. Energy lives in the tiniest and simplest form, the seed atom, as well as in the most complex and most conscious organism which we suppose to be man as an individualized entity. We ourselves are energy, as you presently know. The Return is the return to consciousness of our real selves."

"That marvelous being, Jesus Christ—among other prodigies whom He was nurturing—usually cured with His hands. We know that the hands transmit the energies of the mind. When we place them in the laying on of hands, we are simply extending the healing of the mind. The mind is the wellspring of all healing. When surgeons use their instruments to operate, they intend to cure the body by means of their thoughts, not by their instruments. Consequently when we use our hands in the act of laying on of hands the healing is realized by the mind. In this moment—and this is very important—you ask Father Inti to look with your eyes and touch with your hands to relieve the pain of a brother or sister.

"Jesus was the greatest Illac Uma to come yet to earth. He was also the happiest; He was very joyful. He liked to play with children and to joke with them. He laughed—He was not at all like his sad portraits. The greatest beings are like

23

this—simple and happy. Jesus Christ doubtless earned His title, because a Christ—as you know—is a state of being and not a person. We will develop ourselves spiritually by working within the society in which we live and by serving it.

"Belief does not consist of running to the temple or removing yourself from the temptations of the world in the manner of an ascetic. Belief is not shaving your head or making yourself grow long hair and a hermit's beard. It is not dressing in specially colored costumes such as tunics or cassocks, braids, or showy and conspicuous amulets.

"The only thing that will free us from the limitations that heritage and education have imposed upon us is service—a form of love. Love controls everything. It pushes us towards expansion. Love is life; constriction is death. Appearance is show—nothing more. It signifies nothing. Every day you will see disguised people who love to be regarded as someone important. Now listen: to be Quechua is not a question of wearing sandals or dressing like members of the Brotherhood [2] Only a few among ourselves follow this path of Realization. If we love, fear and sorrow disappear. We have to be free—as free as we wish to be. If freedom is in your mind, you are free. Then, changes will occur on this pilgrimage through life on this planet."

Amaru Cusiyupanqui paused for a minute as if wanting to remember something. Then he continued.

"This extraordinary Being, Jesus Christ, was able to see the past and the future. He had access to these dimensions through the Memory of Nature, the Akashic Records. We consider Him to be an Illac Uma of the third rung. This is the highest known initiation on earth. It is pure Light. It is fusing the self with the Father—with Inti. Such an Illac Uma is more than a true master. He has transcended all of the circles, all spheres of creation."

I did not understand the last part. I interrupted him.

"What is a master? I ask this because you are a master to me."

"A master," he said very seriously, "is a special being. He is a spark of Inti like ourselves but has progressed to the level of masterhood—over a long time[3] and repeated turns of sanctification. He has realized the spiritual force. That is to say, he reached an elevated rank of development. He is a being of our community who—traveling the path of Realization and passing through various initiations—comprehends transcendental knowledge and governs faculties. He understands and comprehends the Light by means of obedience to the cosmic laws. He has transcended the duality of light and darkness, good and evil, sorrow and happiness. He belongs to, and lives on, different stairways of life, e.g., different planes of existence, that is the astral, mental, soulic, and monadic level. He may or may not be in a physical body. If he is incarnated, he is fulfilling a noble mission of helping humanity, with wisdom and consciousness. He serves a greater cause, the Universal Service. He influences the physical and the spiritual planes—transcending our limitations.

"To claim to be a master, as you will understand, means a great deal of pretension. It is very difficult to be a master. Many people wrapped in vanity like to be called such. It is dangerous to enter into such a game. There are but very few genuine masters incarnated upon the earth."

"For me you fulfill these conditions," I thought.

He looked at me, smiled, and stood. Embracing me tenderly, he put his right arm around my back and shoulders and said:

"Let's not discuss what you are thinking. You now know what a master is. You know two of them and I believe that you can differentiate them perfectly.

"Man makes mistakes often; he allows these little bugs, egos, that live with us to rule us and make us believe in anything. Remember—man is not only a physical body; he is basically of the spirit. He is a cosmic being. The material body and its five senses do not limit him. Invisible forces and powers continually help and guide him. However, he is so deaf and blind that he is not aware that this is happening. When he incarnates to earth, he is not aware that he is a transitory visitor. He stays briefly in a

25

body that limits him. Then—conscious or not—he returns to his true existence beyond the physical world. He returns again, reincarnates, to earth at an opportune moment to continue gaining experience. It is also important to know and remember that—in spirit—we descend to earth at the very moment of conception. From that instant we are responsible for the development of our physical bodies, which we usually form in nine months. A long time ago, thousands of years ago, man vibrated and lived, after conception before birth, in perfection in other circles because he breathed with the Creator. Only those who think and act correctly will understand this."

"So, spiritual evolution begins with the fertilization of the egg by the spermatozoa," I thought.

"The evolution of all that exists begins a little further back," he replied. "Some millions of years ago, perfect beings, angels, created by Inti existed who did not know good or evil—that is to say, duality. The Father decided to give them freedom in order to choose. So they committed their first error. He then pulverized everything into very tiny, minute fragments. Thus the fall, the involution, began. During that fall, whenever two tiny particles dashed against each other, they violently repelled each other and almost instantaneously produced spiritual sparks, like artificial fires. Inevitably three fragments collided with each other and bonded. They no longer rejected each other, constituting the first very tiny physical manifestation of life, e.g., the first microscopic atom. The minerals first appeared and…"

"This is somewhat complicated," I thought.

"I will explain it to you again from the beginning. Pay attention and do not get distracted."

He really had patience with me.

Cusiyupanqui picked up a thin stick and wet it in the stream. He used it to point at a river rock. "This cold stone, apparently inert, *has life*," he said with emphasis. "It does not have conscious life since it is missing a lot to complete its mineral evolution. It will evolve to vegetable life and finally animal

26

existence. As you will note, thousands of years remain for it to become conscious."

"How is this, Amaru?" I asked. "Was there only material evolution in all of the kingdoms? What about creation? I know the legend of creation by Wiraccocha."

He interrupted, "Legend as in a story? If you are thinking in this way, you are wrong. For me it is an occult truth. You know the last part; there were up to three creations! I am going to explain to you how it all happened; your opinion is not important. It was like this—you will understand in a minute."

Amaru seemed offended with me for having used the word *legend*.

"I am not offended with you," he replied giving me two taps on my right shoulder with the stick he still had in his hand.

My thoughts did not seem to have any privacy. He grasped all of my thinking. He repeated the creation story. The same thing had happened to me with Nina Soncco. I looked up at him and met his gaze. He smiled and continued talking.

"People waste time verifying what they hear. Truth is like life—like Inti. People may not believe this. Our Father believed it first. Then He permitted evolution."

"In other words there was creation as well as evolution," I said.

"Yes," Amaru said. "In the beginning the Great Infinite Spirit breathed. Millions upon millions of vibrations left His Heart and converted themselves into the first sparks of life in the universe. They awoke little by little to consciousness and took form. Eventually they developed very transparent, subtle, pure bodies. They did not know good and evil. Therefore they only were..." With a tiny wet twig he drew undulating lines on a smooth rock to symbolize this state of angelic being. "Each one of these forms began a specific task in the construction of the universe according to the plans of Inti who watched them for a time. Inti then said *'It is necessary to give them freedom so that they may learn.'* So He

27

gave them freedom. Thus the problems began, and we have continued to create problems until now. When will we learn?"

Amaru said this with an expression of pain and reflection.

"Then Inti was disturbed and destroyed everything. The tradition goes that He converted those first spiritual beings who committed offense into pulverized dust. This dust began to fall—which should be understood symbolically. Whenever two tiny rays of light, e.g., two spiritual particles or molecules, tried to join each other, they violently repelled each other."

"This created involution?" I interrupted.

"Call it what you want," he replied a little bothered. "These rays of light fell in very minute fragments, and they were not able to unite. Until finally a truly, historical-cosmic act came about for the manifestation: two tiny sun rays, particles, that had been crashing and rejecting themselves, combined with a third spiritual particle that also had been falling as a seed atom. They built the first manifestation of matter. Thus physical life began, and the minerals appeared."

He paused as if contemplating a vision of the Akashic Record so that he could better explain it to me.

"Yes, I am seeing something that I will explain to you later. Remind me."

"Yes, Master," I replied with respect and affection.

"The most evolved minerals—in a historically crucial moment after thousands of years in our time—became vegetation; these plants were feeling restless. They did not feel satisfied with themselves. They were anxious to bring forth the animal. After another prolonged era, the most evolved of these plants advanced, becoming the most primitive animals. Evolution continued. After another lapse of time the most evolved animals intended to erect themselves; man was now inherent in the animals, he exerted himself to break the obstacles in order to be born. In time he stood erect. Then man appeared, completing his spiritual structure as primitive man."

"What is this 'spiritual structure'?" I asked.

"Ah, I forgot to explain this part to you," he said. He flung the twig into the stream, as if his forgetfulness bothered him.

"This time, yes, I am bothered with myself," he said smiling and continued.

"The tiny third sunbeam that made possible the union of the other two was a very important key. It was the origin of everything. In recognition of a similar cosmic event, these three elements merge each time a sperm joins an ovum to create new life. That which gives life is the seed that unites the other two. In this seed lies the breath of life. It is this seed atom that constructs and fabricates your physical body based upon the other two.

"This is how man is created. This idea must remain clear—very clear. It begins with the moment of fertilization. Inti, the Sun-Spirit, forms the infant body that a man or woman will use during the stay, the incarnation, on earth. Man is responsible for the body that he will inhabit—no one else is. Understanding this principle will help us to avoid suffering. At the moment of fertilization man also loses memory of life. I am speaking of True Life, not of this fleeting moment of consciousness that passes away on earth.

"This tiny third sunbeam made it possible for all the separated spiritual particles to unite," Amaru continued. "As I told you, they accumulated into bodies—each time more complex. This continued until a particular point in our history was reached, when a ray of sun was needed. Inti breathed this seed atom of light into this intelligence that still was at the animal stage of evolution. This act of Inti made it complete.

"From this instant, the being became primitive man—complete and individualized. He acquired consciousness little by little throughout the eons until today. We are perhaps the most evolved of all creatures on earth. But what a shame! We are also the greatest destroyers."

After a pause he continued. "I referred to this when I mentioned the spiritual structure. The solar rays, that is, the seed atoms, made it possible for these beings to maintain unity in their parts."

I believe he meant force of cohesion or affinity.

"Evolution does not stop. It is always dynamic. The most physically and spiritually evolved men understand what they are about—above all in a spiritual sense." He repeated this last phrase for emphasis.

"In time they will transform into superior humans, super-humans, who will be the future inhabitants of the earth during its next age. As you know, he continues his evolution, and nothing is going to stop him. These new humans will be in harmony with this new state of the world. They will inhabit the earth. Less physical and more transparent, their particles, their atoms and molecules, will vibrate with light. They will have a different structure."

He really surprised me. I did not know. I should have been used to his dissertations. Amaru makes some of his concise explanations in the perfect Spanish that I should speak. He masters languages very well. This issue about languages is another interesting and surprising example of how languages govern. He explained it to me but I did not understand this subject thoroughly. I suppose that if they could master it, I should be able to as well. Others who speak our native tongue can also do this. Quechua is very sweet and expressive. I believe that—yes—Amaru is one of the few super-humans who exist upon earth. He is a living, shining Illac Uma. He is illuminating when he speaks very simply about the topics he is aware of and knows. He expresses such humility and warmth when he refers to Inti, our Father.

He studied me in knowing silence. I gave up pretending that he was only guessing my thoughts.

He continued, "These new humans will occupy a different space-time than ours. They have now started appearing upon earth. This *pachamama* has always suffered a great deal under the abuses of man. There are children who are surprising in their wisdom. Their memory of their past is natural to them. Also, some adults perform extraordinary feats—they are really the new alchemists. At this time there are only a few, although their numbers will increase to help the general evolution."

"And the third creation?" I asked, feeling that I was interrupting him slightly.

"You are in a hurry?" he replied with a light smile. "Walk slowly with all of the energy that you have. You can stumble and fall. Walk slowly. Tread firmly. Urgency does not always mean to run—just as something high is not necessarily superior."

Amaru chided me because I spoke out of turn. I should have waited. When will I learn?

The Master kept on, "When you assimilate all that you hear perfectly, you will come to the secure conviction of what you know—not just of what you are aware. It is very good that you ask questions. The two of us have reunited to learn. I learn from you and you learn from me. The two of us benefit each other."

"I have a great deal to learn," I thought.

"So do I," he said to me. He put his right hand on my shoulder. His eyes shone with much love and tolerance. "You know the last part of creation, which is what the students of history know. They consider it to be a legend, as you said a minute ago. It is necessary to interpret correctly the facts behind the legend. At times we learn things as we hear them; perhaps we do not listen very well. It is necessary to listen to that which is not heard."

How lucky I felt! I had another master—and what a master, thank God!

I said, "Our Master Nina Soncco told me this story. I have also read about it since then in some history books."

"I know that you spend your life reading books." He said smiling. "Men in the second creation received the breath that Inti exhaled. They lived in caves below the earth in darkness. When they learned that Inti had gone, they rebelled. Aware of the rebellion, he destroyed His second generation. Then he sculpted the third creation in stone—a new man. Here we are—without wanting to learn through *K'ullos*. Everything passes by us." He smiled. "I also entertained the thought."

"I do not exactly understand some of this," I said.

"As you will ascertain, this topic is the most external, most visible, part of creation and evolution. I will have to speak to you of other aspects that are slightly complicated and very profound. Perhaps you will not grasp them or they will bore you. However, I will mention one thing to you. The day will come when man—to his level of evolution—will discover and comprehend our level of reality (which is difficult to compass and incredible to believe) with greater amplitude. Our Father Inti is the Black Sun who shines with its own light {see Plate 1}. People want to call Him God, but you know that we also have another name for Him."

I nodded. I know this name.

"His location is in the center of all this." He pointed at the sky to indicate the entire cosmos and the universe. "He is the origin and the goal of creation-evolution. What can I say of Inti? How can I define him? I believe that I would be extremely arrogant and audacious to attempt it. He—simply He—formed different circles of creation from the visible darkness THAT IS."

He stood and picked up another *capulí* stick. He broke off some leaves and drew concentric circles {see Plate 2} and some additional, tiny isolated ones that resembled spheres. This was becoming more interesting; I stood up, too.

"Inti placed His originally created beings on different levels. He meditated on them." He pointed to some of the spheres {see Plate 3}.

"Some beings were more evolved than others. These had the responsibility of directing worlds. Thus, clusters appeared throughout the entire sky." He indicated the circles of creation and the galaxies.

Undoubtedly he was right. As usual, I could hardly believe what I was hearing. I studied him. He was a fellow man; at the same time he was a wise Quechua—equal to Amaru Yupanqui Puma, to Nina Soncco, and to other Illac Umas. I felt unworthy but honored to know them. How could these wise Quechua live such hidden lives that nobody discovered them?

Did I only imagine the village? What about Lucas the Quechua who lived with us?[4] That was real; this had to be a dream. Nobody would believe me. I had the same thought when I was with my Master Nina Soncco. This was incredible. Perhaps I was sleeping.

Plate 1

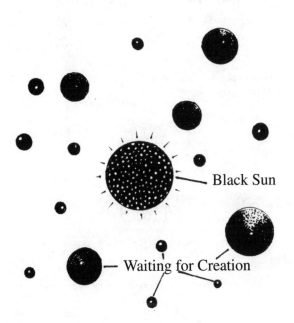

Black Sun

Waiting for Creation

Creation of the Universe

Plate 2

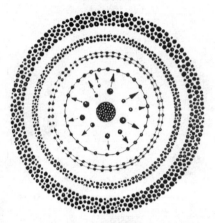

Planes of Evolution

Plate 3

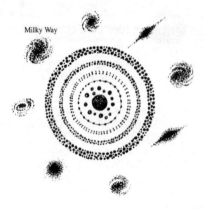

Creation of the Universe and Galaxies

Spheres of Creation! And he was explaining them by drawing with a *capulí* stick on the ground still damp by the morning frost.

I felt very emotional. I prayed, "My Father, YOU know what the truth is. You also know the intention of my writings. It is enough that YOU know…"

"Listen to me. I am not going to repeat myself," said Amaru looking into my eyes. He was a gray-haired giant speaking. "Are you still worried that they will not believe you? Or are you that proud? I am repeating what our Master Nina Soncco has already told you." What humility he had!

"We will not do a thing to help them believe you. Only you are responsible for that. Use your freedom and your liberty with moderation.

"In each world, in each sphere, in each solar system, on each planet like ours, life expresses itself in different ways. It moves with an order and discipline that Inti has arranged. Evolution also manifests itself on different levels according to virtues, which the particles acquire. These contribute to the most complex bodies. They accumulate these particles as they rise. As you know minerals are the basis of all of this construction. Inti is the builder, the Architect of the Universe. All things originate from minerals. They exist on the physical plane successively as plants, animals, and human beings. Because Inti gave freedom to these forms, evolution emerged distinctly in the different worlds, that is, the universes. That is why spheres exist of a very elevated development, such as these." He pointed his *capulí* stick to one part of the circles in his drawing. "Here life develops in total harmony. Look, these are in another time—it is like this everywhere. In this group, our galaxy, look at the location of our solar system {see Plate 4}. It looks like a spiral tail; inside of this tail is our system—very tiny and insignificant. Yet we consider ourselves to be tremendously special. Our haughtiness really slows down the pace of spiritual development. Other worlds are worse than ours. However unlike us, they are working to overcome their state.

35

Plate 4

Solar System

Galaxy of the Milky Way

"Inti gives us a great opportunity at this moment. Progress is necessary. If not, we will have to start over on another dense planet that bears our same present heavy condition.

"The Earth is now preparing itself to pass into a different, more superior state—such as the one I described to you. Its inhabitants will be beings of this higher level. Their bodies will be cleaner and less dense, and they will create harmony in this new land. Therefore, we must use our free will correctly. This is the time to learn discrimination from these other spheres, whose beings knew exactly how to use their freedom. Our planet suffers for various reasons; it would be stupid to repeat them. Evil is not the only cause of suffering; when man fears to recognize good, he also does harm. This night has to pass; the new dawn will be brilliant.

"When we look for what we have lost, we look in the place where we lost it. We look nowhere else. That is mankind's general task at hand. If you lose your keys in the house, why go out to the street to look for them? You will never find them there. You have to look for them inside your house where they are—not outside, I. A. Uma."

He was referring to me! I had been seven years since I heard this name that Nina Soncco and his disciples called me. What emotion this recalled!

"You must work diligently if you desire to advance and avoid returning, avoid further reincarnations. The work— service and research—ought to be your daily activity in order to gain spiritual development. And you know it.

"Good, let us walk a little. I believe that I have talked too much. The day is beginning and there is still much more to say and do." I was not sure what he meant.

We set forth from Samana Wasi in a northerly direction towards the mountains.

I could not, nor should I, squander this opportunity (or any other). I was about to ask more questions without wasting another minute.

However, the Master Amaru Cusiyupanqui spoke with a certain sadness. "We are going to Chupani. This little plateau guards many secrets. I know them and you are partially acquainted with them. Many people are ignorant and will continue to be unaware. In the meanwhile do not speak. You can then comment later."

"I will write it down, Master," I said to him. "You know that Nina Soncco gave me permission. I hope you will also agree to this."

"Yes, you will write in a few more years. It is not your time yet. When the time comes, it will be good for you. People will appreciate your words because you will be expressing the feelings of your heart instead of writing from the intellect. All of the sages—the true masters—lived hidden in this place, in Chupani. They suffered persecution from those Inca who took power by force—who did not yet follow our tradition."

"The sages were the initiated ones," I thought.

"Yes," Amaru answered me, "I believe it is important to remember the meaning of initiation. The term describes itself. It means to go into, to enter, to begin, to start something. That is to say it has a double implication: the entrance into a new place and the origin of a new thing. In antiquity the villages customarily carried a certain ceremony to extremes. This rite admitted a youth into the community of adults."

I wondered, *"Is he referring to the Warachikuy?"*

"For small groups, there also existed another deeper form of esoteric initiation into occult religions, into the mysteries or into mysteriosophic cults—at times you use unusual words to clarify what I am referring to. Although I do not know if they really help," he commented smiling.

"Now the deeper initiation was another matter. It was a process to expand the mind. This entailed study and serious practice of everything that the masters taught. These were the *Ancient Ones*. They allowed the candidate to develop his faculties and elevate his powers. The initiate exerted himself to gain a superior life. He cleansed and purified his mental, moral, and physical vehicles. In this way he accumulated an internal power, which reached such a strength that he would emit a light that was not visible to everyone. When he achieved this, a brother, his instructor, would appear to the initiate. This brother taught him how to use this amassed power. Additional ceremonies may or may not have accompanied this initiation, depending on the occasion. These were secret because of the persecution. Private testings continue even today—in secret or disguised as tradition. However, we have to clarify that the candidate for initiation must earn merit by his own effort. Otherwise he will not experience a single ceremony to teach him how to

38

use the initiatory power. This is true initiation; it will continue being so. We have already told you this, and it is necessary that you always remember it: The first Inca were the last initiates to know of the great mysteries of life and of our royal tradition."

"This indeed is a surprise," I thought.

"Are you surprised because you do not remember?" he asked.

I agreed, nodding my head. *"I do not know why I bother to think in silence. After all, he always knows what I am thinking."*

"Some of the Inca began with ambition. They took power illegally and by force. From that moment, our masters did not initiate them any longer. They only advised the rulers on the best ways to fulfill their duties—advice that the heads of state ignored. The only thing that mattered to them was popularity. Apparently, they had the support of the high priests, who were teachers. Thus, the empire began to decay—the rest is history. The Inca used pressure to learn the secrets that the Brotherhood possessed, but failed. So they seized the Ancient Ones and killed several. They demonstrated the knowledge of power rather than knowledge made into wisdom. Because of this the wise ones had to leave their temples and the Great Sacred City of Cuzco. They had to find refuge in some hidden place where the Inca could not harass them. Thus it was that they left, defended by a regiment of young and loyal people." How important loyalty is!

"They came to the valley of Wilcamayo—the Sacred River." Today it is called Vilcanota; farther to the north it is called Urubamba. "They settled on this tiny plateau called *Chupani* or *Pumacchupan* (the tail of the puma). They lived there for a long time, until their spies told them that they had been discovered. Always protected by their small army, they left for the mountains that you know. That is about it. The mountains were the same that you visited when you went to Village A. The Ancient Ones cautiously established themselves there. I say cautiously because they felt obliged to enact cer-

39

tain rites of protection to ward off persecution and live in tranquillity. There they built a small town."

"How beautiful, a village of masters!" I thought. *"And I was there. What an honor!"*

"These ancient wise ones—our masters—settled themselves and their families on a level area of the terrain. The young members of the army built their houses in a protective circle around the other buildings. Ari Tambowacso led the battalion. He was a young son of the Illac Uma of that era. *Ari* means—among other beautiful things—star. Ari's son's name was (and still is)—you must never repeat nor mention this name, except—you must stop writing now." He gave me an unforgettably severe glance.

"Yes, Master," I said with great emotion, not knowing what attitude to take.

This was incredible. I immediately remembered a vision that I had during a visit to Lake Waypo, situated between Chinchero and Urubamba. I let my mind drift off as if the lake had hypnotized me. I mused at the tiny waves being formed by the breeze. I sat on the shore and lost track of time. It was there that I 'saw' behind me, without turning my head, a young athlete who seemed to be in the Incan army. He bore all of our ethnic characteristics and seemed familiar to me. Whenever I turned to look, the image would disappear from my vision; I decided not to persist. Whom was I seeing? It had a resemblance to, perhaps—

Amaru continued. "So this town grew, preserving tradition and passing it along by word of mouth. Lamentably, many people today do not want to know about their heritage. They are caught up in technology and convenience. Especially our young people are obsessed with the pants they wear. [5] They prefer today's clamorous music. [6] They crave unusual things to distract them. In the cities there are strange notions that confuse them even more. They seem eager to imitate them."

"They do not know that they are lost, Master." I commented.

"That is what worries me. Yes, they are lost and they do not even realize it. They are the descendants of those beings, who were so special. We are not even shadows to the least of them."

I said, "Just think about how great they were, if you and those whom I met are wise! Illac Uma and the true masters are living examples of unselfish love. You demonstrated love by your attitude of giving." He ignored me.

"Few remain," he remarked. [7]

"Each group is more elderly than the last." Here he seemed to recover his enthusiasm. "However, some still listen. They will be the messengers of what is to come, of what now emerges, of events in gestation, of what will truly be a revolution, a change or growth of awareness. It is necessary to clear the way to make room for what belongs in this new era. Much preparation is still lacking for the Aquarian Age. You heard our Master, Nina Soncco. It is necessary to prepare oneself for this moment. We will definitely not come to this event with our physical bodies—or perhaps—one does not know."

"Yes, you know," I thought.

"No I do not know," he replied.

"Are you fulfilling your promises? Are you preparing?"

I demurred. "Well…"

"You do not have to answer," he interrupted (which was fortunate for me). "But yes, it is necessary to remember your responsibilities for the future and for yourself. You are aware; you know what is coming. Does it not seem to be the right moment to participate and share with these people, who search responsibly and sincerely for these truths?"

"Yes, of course, but how do I know whom to—"

Again he interrupted. "There are people who ask with sincerity. They urgently require answers to their doubts. It is necessary to help them. Observe their lives and what they do. Judge if they really at least intend to improve. Besides, I believe that in a few more years you will be able to write; this will help many people. Evidently, you will have to forego some comforts for a while?"

"I will try to be ready for that test, Master," I replied. [8]

"Even though," I continued, "I have trouble finding the

41

exact words to convey the beautiful message that our dear Nina Soncco taught. Knowledge must be useful. Then we can use it in our daily activities to grow spiritually. We cannot just mimic what he taught us."

"This is so. Many people are still prejudiced by appearances, but the destiny of man is defined by something beyond appearance. These people continue to be interested in the external part of knowledge. There is no growth without service. This is the law which transcends humanity and nothing more."

What a beautiful morning! The air was chilly but clear and clean. Like all of the Sacred Valley of the Inca, it was filled with sunlight. Inti sent his first rays. They always arrived late in the morning over Chupani, because it was surrounded by high mountains. We arrived at a small bridge made of tree trunks. We crossed it and quickly climbed the little plateau to its table. Its shape is a triangle facing southeast; streams and rivers run through it. The rivers P'acchac and Sut'uc join exactly at the apex of the triangle. Here was (and will surely remain indefinitely) an enormous rock. It forms a cave that I remember vividly. [9]

"Let us rest a minute," the Master said. "The passing years have taken their toll. I am slowing down. I need to walk carefully in order not to fall."

"You who walked from Village A, which is not exactly around the corner from the Koriwairachina?" [10]

Had he walked? Now I was not so sure.

I said, "You cannot say that the years weigh you down. You are so healthy, they do not seem to have touched you."

Smiling he dismissed my comment and sat down on a level rock.

I will remember this forever. Each time I visit, I can still see him seated there.

He invited me to sit down by his side. I passed him an orange, which he savored with pleasure. After some silent minutes he stood up and gestured for me to follow him. He continued climbing along the left side of the triangle. After we had trudged on for about fifteen minutes, we doubled to the right and crossed over to the other ravine. We continued climbing in silence. I had learned to walk without talking in order to conserve energy. [11] We arrived at a narrow gorge in the cliff. A little path descended to the river P´acchac. The view from this height was breathtaking. Expanses of winter yellow grass surrounded the smooth silence of crystalline water.

We had not yet started the steep path down to P'acchac. I do not know when I dropped my guard—Amaru stumbled. Before I had a chance to catch him he fell, injuring his index finger while attempting to deflect a rock that had fallen on his left hand. I hurried to help him up. The wounded finger had already begun to swell and must have been very painful. He stopped and shook the dust from his clothes. Next he urinated on his sprained finger.

This surprised me.

"You should not be surprised," he said to me with a grimace of pain. "You still have a lot to learn. Anyway, did you not know that urine has curative properties?"

I admitted this. "When I was a boy living in the country, my mother would put some urine drops in my ear every time I had an earache; the pain would go away. We also used it to moisten our hands in winter and for general skin care. I do not know more than this."

"Good, I did not think to talk about it. I cannot imagine why this happened to me, but the accident did occur; nothing is without a cause. I assumed that everyone knew about urine. Therefore, before we descend we will talk about it."

He accommodated himself on the most comfortable rock that he could find. Then, he gave me a seminar on the virtues of this 'refuse'. People in different areas use it in a 'simple way'. Among other uses that Amaru mentioned was the cure for cancer, arthritis, and rheumatism.

Can you imagine? People drink it—you read about such things—they drink it and become rejuvenated. It has been called 'the water of life' very appropriately and with justification. Furthermore, there are books in circulation [12] dedicated to actual research about the properties of urine.

I had lost track of the time. I examined Amaru's wounded finger. The swelling had visibly subsided.

He gripped my left arm firmly to support himself, and he said, "Let us go down. The sun is passing to the other side of the mountain and it will turn cold. We must return to Samana Wasi. Tomorrow, very early, we will return to this quiet pool. Here you will have an experience an event that is necessary after the last seven years."

He said this while walking very slowly. The slope was steep; we had to descend with extreme care—particularly after the accident. We finished the descent and crossed the stream of crystalline ice-cold snow water. I checked Amaru's finger. It was almost normal—the swelling was gone! This time I did not comment.

The return path was smooth, level, and without danger. So being my typically curious self, I felt justified in asking another question.

"What event did you mean, Amaru?"

"Tomorrow, we will speak about it," he replied. We descended to Samana Wasi in utter silence. At home we dined on a very rich, hot vegetable soup. It was good food in the cold weather. Later, while we savored *mate*—tea made from aromatic herbs—he made a comment.

"The human body must always be treated with respect and love so that it does not make us sick. If this does happen—because of age, accident, or neglect—we try to improve its state through mental work. As you know this is the first step that we must learn in order to rule matter in the future. The cause of everything is in the mind; well-managed thoughts will produce very positive effects.

"I want to speak to you about this. Every single cell of your body has consciousness. One must approach it with much love in order to achieve an adequate response. If you 'talk' to it with affection it will respond in the same manner—with love. This requires sincerity and conviction. To-night, make sure that you can do this; tomorrow you are going to need it. For example, if your stomach is malfunctioning: First, try to visualize it, *look* at it in the clearest possible detail. Send it a thought of health and great force—prana—converted into light. You *see* it as though it were completely illumined and brilliant. These little lights are like artificial fires. They softly touch the walls of the stomach and stimulate its integrity. Thus begins its recuperation. Second, you complement this visualization with curative herbs to complete its healing. After this, you may also use other medicines according to the illness, either allopathic or homeopathic medicine. The mental work is the essential thing. The same exercise works for any disease. Besides healing the physical body, it is necessary to maintain constant control of oneself. Also, you have to be vigilant of your light, your health aura, so that your body responds adequately when it is needed.

"Your body can adapt to (among other things) different temperatures. For example, the body can feel warmer than the winter air or cooler than a suffocating summer. Practice will guide you to control your body adequately. People feel cooler or warmer according to the thoughts they have at that moment. You can apply this principle to everything. It will help you a great deal in your daily activities. Deep in the subconscious mind, people have multiple values of cold and hot which are not conscious. Therefore, one needs to take care of the 'deep' in order not to have thoughts that may afterwards cause us harm. Everything is outwardly mental, meaning conscious, or deeply mental, meaning subconscious. The body responds to a given order. It responds better to love. It is necessary to learn how to give love."

"Well then, explained in this way, it seems simple," I commented.

"It is, if you dedicate a few minutes of daily practice to it," the Master said. "It is clear that you do not have much time before tomorrow. You will have to quickly reflect and meditate over everything that you have heard. I cannot explain more to you."

"However," I said, "I believe that you can tell me what we will do tomorrow in Chupani."

"In order to learn how to swim, you have to throw yourself into the water. You should take all the appropriate precautions, of course. You do not want to drown, right?" He watched me. "Therefore, tomorrow you will throw yourself into the water in order to learn."

I did not understand his allusion. That beautiful pond was not deep enough for swimming. I had to wait until tomorrow.

We went to sleep.

The Second Day

I could not sleep well. I passed the night (at least I thought I did) trying to remember all of Master Amaru's words.

At some point, I vaguely remember dreaming about the stream of crystal-cold water. Somehow it changed into a deep, overflowing river. I sank in the water all the way up to my neck. I tried to save myself by dog-paddling, but I could not touch the bottom. Then something stopped me. I was immobilized. I could not move my arms or legs. I wanted to leave, but I had no physical form. Then—I am not sure how it happened—I saw myself stretched out on the grass—and I woke up.

It was still dark. I had no idea what the hour was. Daybreak would be a long time coming. I did not like my dream. It probably resulted from what Amaru had said to me the previous day.

Daylight finally arrived. It promised to be a very clear day, so I arose.

I found Amaru—well-protected in his poncho—waiting for me outside my parents' house. I embraced him, and we immediately set out for Pumawanca to beat the sun to Chupani. We did not climb the small plateau. We followed the path to the right until we arrived at the pond.

To my surprise, eleven *Ancient Ones* awaited us there. *Ancient One* is a figure of speech; none of them appeared to be over fifty or sixty years old. With Amaru there were twelve. They were all Quechua, and greeted him in the customary way. They ignored me. I greeted them in a loud voice; they answered courteously but no one looked at me. Amaru Cusiyupanqui took off his poncho. Everyone followed his lead. Amaru remained standing as they formed a circle around me and sat down on their ponchos. The Master gave me an order.

"Take off all your clothes."

"What?" I said confused. "Undress myself?"

"Yes, undress yourself," he affirmed severely.

I have always prided myself on being a quick to understand.

47

I had no alternative and nothing further to say. I stripped till I was naked in the hour of tremendous cold that always precedes the arrival of the sun (not to mention that it was full winter).

"Get into the river," was Amaru's second order. He looked very serious.

So I did. I stepped into the chill of an iceberg—this was my impression. With their shoes still on, everyone else entered the water. I say this because I was barefoot.

"Lie down." Amaru faced me with his third order. He seemed very sure that I would obey.

Could I do it? I wavered, but they did not give me time to react. They seized me and plunged me in to my neck. They held me down in a horizontal position; my feet went in the direction of the current. I felt like I was turning into an 'ice cube'. I was about to shout with pain from the intense cold when I heard mantric singing. Yes, it was a mantra. It impressed me tremendously. From that instant on I felt nothing more—neither cold nor hot. I remained floating with my mouth open. I looked at them. They looked back at me very seriously and used their feet to keep me in place so that the current of the water would not drag me along. While repeating this rare melody—strange and mysteriously pleasing to the ear—they formed a circle around me in the river. I am unsure about what happened after that. They seemed to be very far away, as if they had moved away while they sang. The truth was that they were standing right there unmoving.

Something happened in my mind; my eyes obeyed. They lifted me up. I felt as though I were an iceberg. How much time had elapsed?

They stretched me out on ponchos spread over the grass. They covered me with others. They stroked all of my body. I only watched. I could not move one limb. It was as though I were hypnotized.

Then they placed me on my feet. They gathered up their ponchos and formed another circle around me. I felt heat—as if there were some stove nearby. My body felt no heaviness; in fact, I did not seem to have a body at all! I floated and saw the others from above. They were aflame with a light that issued forth from their shoulders. Imagine the sun just beginning to appear molten behind a mountain. That was the intensity of this light, which became very bright. It bothered my eyes. I could not see the men. Everything shone.

I experienced a series of extremely beautiful, indescribable things. I could see all of the Chupani plateau. A very bright point of light shone from a river that crossed a wide field covered with grass. It was them!

I began to cry. I heard a voice (it seemed to be mine) saying, "From the start without beginning, from your appearance without birth. Float and revolve through the spaces created and not created before the Beginning. This is the point of departure of the visible and invisible." I do not remember anything else I said. I was very emotional. So much kindness surrounded me! So much love enveloped me, without my deserving it! So much came to me without my having given anything! This was exceptional treatment for me without being one of them—but that must be it! What a responsibility this was!

I touched the earth. The grass was still humid.

Amaru ordered me to dress. Then he gave me a hug. His hug was filled with a love that was very expansive and visible in the other masters. I tried to respond in the same manner. All of them followed suit. Fresh in this solemn moment they looked at me and directed some words of happiness after embracing me.

"I thought for a moment that you would not survive," Amaru said to me. "There is the possibility of going over to the other side during these trances. It has happened before."

"I also thought that I was dying," I replied with tears still in my eyes. "But here I am. It seems that I must still continue for a good long time?"

At that moment an older woman arrived. She was Amaru's wife—with a very beautiful smile on her lips! She held a *p'ucu* full of a very hot liquid, which she gave to me to drink.

It may have been the same concoction that she gave me the first time. It was a very pleasing tea of aromatic herbs.

Everyone sat down, and we shared corn toast with the *mate*. After drinking and eating, I approached Urpi[1], the wife of Amaru Cusiyupanqui. I embraced her, and kissed her with all of the love I was feeling. She responded to me in the same fashion. Urpi was pure within; her black, brilliant eyes gave a sweet look. She reminded me of Nina Soncco's wife, except Urpi was slightly taller. She invited me to sit beside her.

Urpi took my hand affectionately and said, "Happily, you have passed the ordeal. We were worried."

As I sat there, two pretty young women and one boy appeared. I could not tell you how they arrived. They had adorned themselves in beautiful attire of typical vivid Quechuan colors. These were clothes of celebration—considered very special to accompany a very distinguished event.

Behind them followed three young men equally costumed. They carried flutes, bagpipes, a drum, and something else that they placed beside Amaru. The Master pulled out another flute from under his poncho. He began to play a melody that gave me goose bumps. It was profoundly sad and very powerful. His was a flute solo to shake the whole canyon of Pumawanca. People must have heard it for a great distance.

We all listened in silence. The music changed imperceptibly. At the same time its volume fluctuated; it faded until it was nearly inaudible; a moment later a blaring bagpipe behind me made me jump with surprise. All the while the flutes continued very softly in a melodic trio that steadily grew louder. The young women began to clap; the boy moved in cadence to the rhythm that had just begun (also softly). Again the sharp sound of Amaru's flute sliced the atmosphere but with another rhythm. It seemed to be a *huaino* rhythm with an African flavor. The dancer began to clap with vigor; the young women joined the dance.

How beautiful! Never had I seen such a lovely ritual dance! The three dancers clapped; Amaru kept time with his legs. He gave the impression that he might also dance at any moment, although he never actually did so. Everyone became infected by this strange melody. I also began to move. One of the young women took my hand and tugged me very gently to the bank of the river.

"Not again!" I thought as she gave a little push.

Her act was symbolic; the purpose was to put my feet in the river. A moment later the other young woman stretched out her hand to me to help me back onto the bank; she used a beautiful gesture of protection. How impressive this double ritual was! Then the two joined their arms—keeping me in their center—while they continued dancing. I felt transported to Village A. In that instant I had the first thought straight from a vision. I felt dizzy.

The music turned from sad to very happy. It was inviting me to see everything with abundant color, happily, optimistically, and with a zest for life. The two young women took my hands and conducted me to Amaru's side.

The music and the dance continued—for how much longer I cannot say. The volume softened while everyone who performed stole away behind some trees. I saw them no more. The musicians and dancers were gone. What a gift they had given me! Silence enveloped me. Amaru meditated in some far-removed thought for a few minutes more. Then he stood up. He spoke very seriously and affectionately.

"This was a exceptional act for a special son and brother. We will also consider this day to be extraordinary from now on. As of today, June 22, you will establish Samana Wasi!"

I was stunned; many reactions roiled within me. A lump rose in my throat; I felt unable to breath or cry until I burst into a flood of endless tears like a child. They hugged me again—the twelve who were the only ones remaining there. I could not bear to take leave of Amaru's wife Urpi.

Amaru let some time elapse before he said, "We must depart."

"Must you go so soon?" I asked extremely grieved.

"They are returning to the Village. They only came down for this event," Amaru said. "You and I will go down to Samana Wasi. We still have to discuss various topics. We must clarify our points of view, since we always respect each other's opinion."

Sad and grateful at the same time, I had to bid farewell to each of them. Each one at a time gave me a good-bye hug that only the *Ancient Ones* know how to give. They left for the mountains that were too high for the abundant vegetation of this zone below the small plateau.

Amaru and I arrived at Samana Wasi. The sun had passed mid-day. We ate sparingly. The Master whom I trusted utterly, rose and went out to the garden. Despite the harsh winter, the hydrangeas, that my mother had cultivated with much love since my youth, were still blooming beside some other flowers.

"Are you reminiscing about your mother? You were thinking about her," he said to me when I joined him.

"Yes Master. She is living in Cuzco. Her health is a little delicate and I am worried."

"You know, we all have to leave at some time or other. You must understand this in order to be more tranquil," he said. "I do not mean that your mother will die now. We suffer for lack of understanding. Keep this in mind: When we understand, suffering disappears. Understanding does not mean a lack of love.

"Your parents will arrive today," he said with satisfaction.

"But they only know that I was coming—not that you would be here. I did not tell them anything. Should I have informed them?" I asked.

"Of course, it's obvious. You would not have mentioned me. You doubted my visit in Ccusilluchayoc," he said smiling. "Your father knows that I am here. They will arrive this afternoon.

"These flowers are lovely—so are those," he remarked, caressing the hydrangeas and roses. "They are happy in our company."

"Why not," I thought, *"with such a visitor!"*

"They sense us; we likewise can feel them. You know that it is possible to convert oneself into plants, animals, and even into rocks?" he asked.

"I have heard something about this, "I remarked, "but…"

"Let me explain," he interjected. "We do not change ourselves to become these things. The process of completely

52

transforming into them would almost mean returning to the past, would mean an involution. This process has not been done for many thousands of years.

"It means something different to enter their bodies and experience their senses. It requires great dedication and conviction of what one intends to do. If we *enter* a condor by invocation, we transpose ourselves into him. We feel the wind with the sensation of gliding through the air. We search for food when he is hungry. From the heights we enjoy the vast panorama of the valleys and the landscape. We also gain a different perspective and a different idea of liberation. We will feel his heart beating and his lungs working. The same process occurs if we *convert* into a puma. His ferocity and his olfactory sense will become our characteristics. Do you understand?"

"I am trying to understand, Master. "I replied.

"It is entering into harmony with all of the cells of that body," he continued. "It is demonstrating love and respect."

"With this master," I thought, *"I must be very attentive. I shall have to observe his attitudes in order to learn. Otherwise he will be surprising me with his words every moment."*

"This is so. It is necessary to always be attentive and to expect the unexpected in any circumstance," he explained. "The art of moving objects, that is, telekinesis, shares similarities with the converting technique. There are some additional details to learn in its practice (or in synthesis). We must enter into harmony with an object so that it responds to our requirements. The conviction and love that you place in the object will help the movement. Do not forget—everything has life."

"What about people like ourselves? I mean—can this also work on plain, ordinary humans who make up the majority of our population?" I asked. "Can we enter into their bodies?"

"Of course. This happens in special cases and with as much respectability as it has had in the past. I want to say that we should pay courtesy to the privacy of a brother of our level.

Only *enter* him to help him; we should not do this to simply satisfy our curiosity. To so *convert* oneself into a brother or sister exacts a great deal of responsibility. Luckily, it is not easy to do this.

"You already know that there is much difference and distance between having knowledge and ability, that is, to truly know. This is not possible for everyone. We still tend to abuse power and profit from it. Therefore, we require certain conditions.

"Some people (for karmic reasons) are born with *advantages*, for example paranormal faculties, although they lack sufficient character development to use them wisely. They have the opportunity to overcome their problems by putting these abilities to good use. Sadly, most of them fail this excellent chance at growth; they lose it through vanity and abuse of their gifts. The debt they accumulate is tremendous. They will live paying and will die owing. It is one thing to have *advantages* in addition to spiritual maturity; it is another to have it as a karmic condition. Not all people who have *advantages* are spiritually developed. We avoid mistakes if we take this into account."

"I know people—a good number of them—with some paranormal gifts," I commented. "They behave disastrously. It is obvious; there is a large difference between saying and doing—between appearance and being—between high living and living in superiority. We make mistakes; we deceive ourselves and others. This life is not worth the pain of living this way! One cannot just exist and die on such a beautiful planet. We have to change. If we seek and desire to grow, we urgently need honesty, honor, and cleanliness in action."

Amaru said, "To orient our lives with precision, we must first ask ourselves what we want. What do we want for ourselves without being self-centered? We should feel at peace with what we want and do. This attitude will overflow to benefit all that we love and all who are near us. Then we will feel very well; we will feel free to

54

act without pressure; our surroundings will not suffocate us.

"It is sad to feel cheated by not fulfilling our dreams. We can actualize the feeling of satisfaction by knowing what we want. We will feel harmonious with ourselves; we will discover our mission that (this time) is a responsibility towards others—since you know that life is fundamentally service."

"If we were to comprehend this action in human relations, we would all be quick to help each other. What a tragedy that this is not the case!" I thought.

"Leave me alone for a minute," he said to me. I did so.

The sun set, and the day came to an end. We were soon to enter the obscurity of the night. I walked with haste toward Animasniyoc or Almacunayoc[2]—today known as Samana Wasi. It is located behind my parents' home.

Even though I was awake, I began to dream. The morning's events had struck me tremendously and promised to mark me for my entire life. I can still recall this sensation of emptiness—weightlessness. Finally, something cosmic happened to me. I saw a vision of what would soon be reality. Abandoned children and elderly adults would no longer be homeless. They walked and played happily. They would be no less than a perpetually growing family without any exclusions. I *saw* the gardens and the modules for the children's living quarters. These were in front of the large house that would be the first building. More houses down the slope would be homes of the elderly. The area seemed sufficiently large but *seeing* it in this manner showed me that I was not going to attain the goal. I lacked enough acreage for a small pool, a small multiple-use field for the children to play games and sports. It did not cost me anything to dream. Ah! This was a subject of pressing meditation. At first we could shelter the adult volunteer helpers in the large house[3].

"I am sure that you will achieve this." Amaru surprised me. He had come up unexpectedly, as usual. "Inti will always help you."

"Yes, Master," I said to him, "we will achieve the goal with complete confidence. We will undertake this work of good with much love and without any hidden agenda. We will break ground on June 22, as you suggested this morning."

"That is a very important date, it is the winter solstice," he said. "We will discuss the various reasons for it at some later time."

"We have the support of all of you and of God," I said. "It cannot fail. We have grasped our mission. We must do it with a responsibility for humanity. From here will come forth a new human being. He will exercise complete balance and harmony. His faculties will be open for service and the elderly will still feel useful. They will live happily to their last days.

"The volunteers at Samana Wasi will serve a great purpose, though they will not be aware of it. They have no idea of its potential magnitude. They also have to envision man's role in the coming new era—as you say. Samana Wasi must nurture the development of a humanity which is different from today's normal standard. Its *advantages* will be available for use for the good of all and will have a highly developed spiritual nature. Children will come to live here for two reasons. Some will surely be obligated by their former debts, their karma. Others will be old souls who return to earth, reincarnate, to carry out a mission that benefits all of humanity. As you will see, the work is very serious, arduous, and of total transcendence. This is no game or hobby that you develop here. There will also be all kinds of difficulties. Do not forget that the elderly who will reside here will also bring their talents, karma, and other motives to Samana Wasi. It will be a center that radiates ideas. Similar places on earth will establish such services in order to aid the helpless. This must not be just an ordinary house for the abandoned. It has to be a family; all of those who work with you must understand this.

"Dear Master," I said with gusto, "we are claiming all of these things. Without bragging, this has been our intention all along. We do not seek to promote ourselves, nor do we desire publicity. Why should we want it? I believe that we have finally reached a level of consciousness that allows us

56

to work without self interest. In time this will become reality. We know what we want."

"Yes I know." He always had an answer. "People will come to join you. They will be brothers and sisters who also need to experience the goodness in your spiritual belief. Many of them will come without knowing why. Nevertheless they will share former relationships, e.g., past lives, with the children, the elderly, and particularly with you. You will feel this but do not need to tell them. Several of them will find themselves. They will discover who they are."

"How important that is!" I thought.

"Others will lose their opportunities. They will simply withdraw from Samana Wasi. Very few volunteers will recognize each other from past lives. It will depend on the work that they will do. There will be no lack of curiosity seekers and critics; they will lose interest quickly."

"That is good," I thought.

"We will include and serve everyone."

"Does that mean that everyone will have the opportunity?" I asked.

"Yes, we hope that most of the residents will properly progress in life during their time in Samana Wasi.

"Let us rest. It is dark already, and the air is a little cold."

"Not as cold as the dawn was," I thought.

Amaru looked at me, smiled, and softly touched my face. I felt his tremendous energy as if It had shaken me.

We returned to my parents' house. They had already arrived! I hugged them. I was not expecting such a pleasing surprise.

"I will never learn. The Master had known they were coming. How long will I live with these doubts? Each step that I take confirms his wisdom," I thought.

"Do not worry," Amaru told me while he hugged my mother and then my father. The Master greeted them very congenially. "Now you will learn. You are imperfect. Doubts can help you to arrive at the truth."

My mother invited us to sit on the porch while she brought us a pot of chocolate. It was a strong chocolate made especially for the cold weather. I burned my tongue and Amaru laughed like a child.

These people are really very special. They laugh like any ordinary soul. They enjoy hearing and telling jokes. They light up when they teach—unlike others who teach very seriously because they assume that they should put on a certain manner. Their faces do not know how to laugh. They are exclusive about the people they contact and snobbish about who may approach them. How distant they are from being true masters!

After drinking carefully, he acknowledged the hospitality and then rose to retire.

"I must tell you that your presence honors me." I said to him. "Thank you for everything that you gave me. I do not deserve it."

I went to bed. This had been another day of many emotions and lessons. It had all been like a dream and I needed to be alone in order to reflect on these ephemeral events. I felt compelled to ponder everything and to be as candid as possible. As I drifted off to sleep, my thoughts wandered at will.

I have to feel this love—the *Ancient Ones* not only discuss it; they demonstrate it every minute. This feeling must rise up from a deep reflection on the significance of life—on our unique origin. I can now better understand the traditional Vedic credo. Amaru makes evolution seem simple when he explains it:

"The Vedas teach that a God-atom sleeps in each stone. It then awakens in each plant. It stirs with movement in each animal. It thinks in each human. It loves in each angel. From this principle, we conclude that we should respect each stone as if it were a plant, each plant as if it were an animal, each animal as if it were a human being, and every human being as if he were an angel.

"An angry person undoubtedly loses his struggle. We often become angry through shallow thinking; this can rapidly grow into hate, and he who hates is disgraced.

"Our work must have beauty; it will be written with the heart and it will be read in our results.

"If I want to read my own 'inner book', I have to begin a true meditation. I need to *be*. I need to enter universal consciousness with spontaneity and freedom. I should now allow the glamour of paranormal phenomena or other fashionable ideas to influence me.

"The gate to the true path will open when these teachings bear fruit in experience. This is the fruit of acting on one's convictions and of serving others.

"We need to learn acceptance and understanding of ourselves as people. We need to define ourselves so that we can love ourselves as we are. When we clear the past through our actions, we will truly lead our own lives."

Perhaps all of these thoughts flowed from my mind, desperate for understanding or possibly someone said them to me. I might have heard them in a dream, such as the dream that was just beginning to overtake me.

The Third Day

The third day was beautiful—cold but dry. The air was extremely pure. The sun illuminated the morning sky brightly, even though it was yet to emerge from behind Tantanmarca.[1]

I found Amaru Cusiyupanqui standing on a little stone bridge. He was gazing at the mountain while waiting for sunrise. It was eight o'clock in the morning. Without looking at me, he sensed my approach from behind and began to walk toward Samana Wasi, and so I hurried my pace to greet him. He answered in Quechua and asked if I had slept well.

"Yes, Master. I did sleep soundly. Thank you, why do you ask?"

"I *saw* you were very restless in your bed. Then, you left your body. You were staggering everywhere without direction." A light smile played on his lips.

I watched him. He was well covered. The day was undoubtedly going to be cold. He wore a purple poncho with green rays—the colors contrasted very attractively. It was so large that it covered him to the calves. His classic *ch'ullo* covered his gray hair.

"Well," I answered, "I suppose I am not conscious during these trips. Besides, yesterday was such a special day for me that I could not fall asleep right away."

"Before sleeping," he said, "you should choose what you want to investigate while your body is resting. Your desire to explore something should be sincere and not mere curiosity. When your intention is correct, the response is always clear. People have brought back many innovations from these *journeys.*"

"This is so, Master—this is so. Amaru, my dear Master, our language, our mother tongue, is very expressive and sweet. It expresses much warmth in what one wishes to say. The result is that each sentence is completely clear."

"I want to remind you," he said. He seemed particularly attentive—more so than at other times. He definitely wanted to confirm something. "The mother tongues (in order) are

61

Quechua, its brother language Aymara, and another ancient earth language. This third language was spoken by men who cut their hair—they completely shaved their heads—and wore large, colorful robes. They are the source of all other languages."

"Are you referring to Sanskrit?" I asked. He had surprised me again.

"Yes, the same," he replied.

"I hope I understood correctly! Quechua, Aymara, and Sanskrit. They are the origin of all the languages of earth? This is just too much. If it's true, it's incredible!"

Amaru was telling me this in two languages. He handles Castilian[2] very well. When he needed to explain something exactly and clearly, he used only Quechua—*Runasimi*—the language of man.

This confirms some ideas of my own. Though, I do not know what to think. Amaru mentioned that I had not been willing to accept this information for a long time. I had read about such a language theory in some books about Perú, Bolivia, and Ecuador, and yet this seemed to be an extreme conjecture. Now Amaru—the last known incarnated Illac Uma of our Brotherhood and beautiful tradition—affirmed it and confirmed it. I had no more doubts!

Many Quechuan words exist in Sanskrit; Quechua shares the roots of many other languages. Take for instance the Quechua word *samana*. It exists in Sanskrit and is pronounced with an accent on the first syllable. It was Quechua first, then Aymara, and finally Sanskrit. When it returned to the Andes as Spanish, the Spaniards took credit for the word. Sometimes I have mused about this; at times I would say, "Our history will soon be written."

I believed in a utopia born of the Andean heat, which runs through my veins. I have spoken with linguists more than once and, as connoisseurs of Sanskrit and other languages, they told me that Quechuan words and roots exist in other languages. Karola Sieber is a (regrettably) little-known German researcher, who found a village in Turkey whose natives spoke Quechua. Unfortunately, I do not remember the title of her book.

I said, "If our language is that ancient, and if it came first, where did the first human appear? Here?"

"Yes—definitely yes—but it is necessary to explain the background, since the story is still unknown. However, it will be discovered soon. Our past will approach us from the distance. Many occult mysteries remain on the invisible dimensions of our Planet. The consciousness of man surges ahead. The sleeping memories in his subconscious mind are already approaching.

"For a while, some people will ridicule your assertions. Others will read with scruples—and this is good. These people do not blindly accept what that they don't know. Humble people will consider it worthy of further study or research. Pride and its companion, envy, are widespread.

"Do not worry; go ahead and share your knowledge. Whoever is ready will understand and accept it in silence. Other things will cause a tremendous revolution of consciousness and attitude. What would you say if I told you that the language of Adam and Eve—the first humans, according to the Bible, that appeared upon earth—was Quechua!" He laughed heartily at me.

I lost my breath.

"It is possible. Yes, why not? I believe that anything is possible," I thought. Nothing ought to surprise me after everything I saw and heard—what these beautiful Quechua masters taught me.

"Then, is this the Garden of Eden?" I asked with dread.

"Now, you draw your own conclusions," he said smiling.

South America enjoys a unique reputation in the world. Archeologists have found some unusual myths concerning the creation of man. The root word for man implies a human being. It turns up frequently. For example, Brazil has the words

Manaos, Manoa, and *Manus* (which is the name of the very first man). The famous park Manú is an extensive ecological preserve between Cuzco and Madre de Dios in Perú. I read a book or heard some lectures about this subject, but I did not pay due attention to those experts, who presented their knowledge with much warmth and sincere enthusiasm.

The name Perú reportedly means paradise. It is a derived from the old name *Piru*—the rugged region that extends from Quito, Ecuador to the south of modern Perú. Besides, Perú in ancient Wanca means park, garden, or luxuriant vegetation. The Sanskrit word *péru* means paradise and Sun. In Waraní *para* is the word for forest, lush vegetation, or orchard. It relates to the words Perú, Péru, or Piru. The Greek word *paradeisos* has two parts. *Para* means park, small forest, or garden. *Deídoo* means to inspire fear, respect, veneration. According to legend, one of the four rivers that surrounded Paradise was *Perat*—another word related to Perú.

Several devotees of broad and unprejudiced sociology affirm that migrations probably passed from America, to diverse parts of the world, and back to America during thousands and thousands of years. They also hold that the origin of the principle races is on this continent. According to this information the Wanca were a nation that extended through all of the continents. Their ethnicity adapted to different climates. All the diverse variations of skin color originated from America. The Wanca had white complexions. They acquired other names in different places where they settled, but they were the same race. We might know them as *Kunos* , that is, Huns, *Karios, Arawakos,* Scythians, and Moguls. People usually confuse the Aryan designation with the white complexion. A well-read person inadvertently told me that the American civilizations had been Aryan—that is to say they practiced the cult of the Sun. Aryan comes from *aru,* which means sun or star. The *ari* (cone) is a symbol for the sun. It depicts a ray of light and life that descends to earth.

Of course! Now I remember two American philologists. One is Bolivian and the other is Ecuadorian. Emeteri Villamil de Rada wrote *Amáraka, Mundo Sin Tiempo (America, World Without Time)*. Héctor Burgos Stone wrote *La Lengua de Adán (The Language of Adam)*. How interesting these books are! Both books have high reputations and I read them with a great relish and love; in some way they confirmed what Amaru had taught me years before.

"Good, now listen to me," said Amaru, drawing me out from my reverie. "What you are remembering is factual. Your reasoning did not allow you to accept these and other truths. You thought that they were audacious and taboo."

"Fanatical," I thought.

"Yes, I can never remember this word—fanatical, you say?"

"No, I did not say," I thought, *"but with you masters it is the same. You always know what I am thinking,"* I hoped that he thought this was funny.

He ignored my thoughts that time and continued to speak on the main subject.

"The great roads that are attributed to the Inca cross all of Perú and beyond. They already existed before the Inca."

"What about the sanctuaries of Machu Picchu and Sacsaywamán?" I asked.

"It is obvious that they were also there before the Inca," he said with emphasis. "There is a gap in the history that we learn in school. There is, well, an enormous time discrepancy between the civilizations of the Wanca, the Quechua, the Aymara who were much earlier, and the Inca. No one has completely investigated this. For a true discovery the seeker has to be completely sincere and humble in order to accept what he finds. Rather soon these mysteries will come to light.

"The earliest Inca—as you know—were the last people initiated in the great truths. Those who followed them immediately lost the knowledge. They did not rise to understanding the marvelous wisdom of our predecessors—our true ancestors. Because of this, we Quechua zealously guard what we learned from oral tradition. The Inca maintained and practiced the shallowest traditions. They inherited some ceremo-

65

nies and rites from their grandparents, which were not the authentically powerful ones.

"I know that you worry about what I am saying. It grieves me, but you have to speak the truth. They will not believe you. Many years will pass before you gain credibility—perhaps even after you have gone."

I thought, *"Wisdom is implicit in all of the beings of nature. Our immediate ancestors lost their cosmic-cultural birthright. Nevertheless, something must have remained in their genetic memory. Perhaps there are other hermetic groups besides these wise Quechua. The people who live throughout the entire Andean range might keep this wisdom alive."*

"This is right," he said, breaking into my speculation. "Scattered throughout the Andes, the knowledge is alive. Other groups constantly visit us in order to maintain relationships. They receive instruction and teach us how they live this Great Truth. Sadly, the original information has altered subtly each time it has changed hands, according to the notions of the custodian who passed along the knowledge. This was ordained to obstruct a man who might want to arrive at the fountain of knowledge."

"I had observed something about this once in a while," I said, "and now I see it more clearly. All over the earth, it seems that there was only one master who taught the sciences and arts. The megalithic structures left everywhere have many similarities. The resemblance is surprising. For example, I have heard that the Etruscans in Italy were a branch of the Wanca. The Pelasgians were also Wanca. They established settlements in Greece. All of them left colossal works for our admiration. Only one hand has sculptured the *moais* of Rapa Nui (Easter Island), the giants of Tiwanacu and the faces of the sculptures of Marca Wasi. How exhilarating this thought is!

"Knowledge is only one whole. I agree with the Dalai Lama, the Buddhist monk, the Catholic priest, the Christian, the Mohammedan, the Egyptian, the Quechua, the Lanka, the

66

Aymara, and the Incan: God, our Father Sun, is everywhere. This truth comes to us from the most distant nations. How vast this work is! When mankind is free, politics and religion will not be able to separate us. Man will be completely revolutionized by giving birth to something that is at the same time new and very ancient."

"You seem to be certain of what you are saying," he observed. "That is good. It will help you a lot when you write and speak.

"Earth is not a pile of things. It is a synthesis of everything. We have to learn to take care of it, to enjoy its beauty, and to be happy. Luckily, all of the sadness and the ugliness that we experience does not last. Beauty and happiness are eternal in our lives. I remind you that Noccan Kani gives you security. There is no sadness. There is no fear. Paima Kani is happiness—the eternal expression. It is the place without death—of Noccan Kani."

He paused briefly, as if giving me time to assimilate—to better digest what he had told me. Then he continued, "Let us say that it is most probable that all the inhabitants of earth—white, black, red, or copper—that is to say the Germans, Italians, Greeks, Asians, Africans, and all the other ethnic variations—are branches from a common Andean trunk of the Wanca, Quechua, Aymara. Our vocabulary lives in all of these languages—with some variations but still the same. We belong to this root.

"It is a very great honor to be born Andean. We have earned the right. We will accomplish the dedicated mission that many still do not understand—TO SERVE. We must serve, I. A. Uma!" He called me for the second time by the affectionate expression that the *Ancient Ones* gave me many years ago. Hearing it again, I became very emotional.

"The community is our obligation and our responsibility. We must serve it. As you have already heard various times, it begins with taking care of yourself. Only then will you learn to serve others with warmth and with tenderness. All over America there are vestiges of our race. The members of our brotherhood come this way from Perú, Bolivia, Ecuador, Paraguay, Brazil, Argentina, Chile and everywhere."

"To Cuzco, to the Sacred Valley of the Inca, or to Village A?" I wondered.

He watched me. "I already told you; they go to the village. All of them already know about the great event that approaches. As you said, it will be a true revolution. We have to prepare ourselves.

"Well, let us end this for now. They are calling us to lunch."

My mother appeared. She had the personality of a *mamá:* we left immediately to have lunch!

While we walked back to the house he continued, "Our language will not die. No language dies. It changes and continues by other names as do the people who speak them."

My mother was an affectionate woman, but she demanded immediate obedience to her orders. The food was very pleasant as always. Then, she rose to make the coffee. I followed to help her. When I returned, my father's eyes had filled with tears. He tried to hide them, but it was too late. I saw but pretended not to notice. What had he and Amaru talked about? Father would eventually tell me after a few months.

Amaru missed nothing. As if returning to this morning's theme he said, *"Runasimi* is thus the primordial language. It is the language of man—the main language—the language of mankind. It is spoken in Perú and in America."

"It is the Aryan language," I commented, "that is to say, of solar or stellar derivation?"

"Yes, it is wholly solar," he said getting up from the table. He thanked my parents for their hospitality, and we left.

We sat on the stairs in front of the main door. He remained quiet. I had the impression that he wanted to be quiet.

I withdrew unobtrusively and went off to reflect on what I had heard that morning. It had been a morning filled with light, with surprised worry, and with much responsibility. Our origin was in this very place! At least that is how it seemed.

I sat on a rock at the edge of the stream that ran behind my parents' house opposite the kitchen. I meditated on the flow-ing water. Dry leaves floated lazily by as I gazed into the crystalline current. I used to play here in my youth; I sailed pieces of wood down the stream and race them with one another.

A very important framework was embedded in our legends. God created man in America—in South America. Was it in the Sacred Lake or near it? How much Amaru has given me! What did he say to my father? What worried both of them so much that they kept their silence? Their faces were not as joyful as they had been in the previous two days. They did not look sad, but they seemed worried. It may have been a purely human problem. This white-haired Quechuan man was wise. What else was going to happen?

I felt a hand on my left shoulder. It startled me; I had not felt it coming.

"I surprised you," he said softly.

"Water is the road. Do not forget—it is life. It is necessary to use it justly and with affection. You will see how it responds to you. If the torrent tumbles down with force, it will pass over the earth that you wish to irrigate. It will escape and scarcely moisten the land. It will not penetrate it. Allow it to slowly trickle little by little, without such fury. It will thoroughly saturate the earth, which then bears the fruits of life.

"This resembles an impetuous man who wants everything immediately. He thinks and demands. He must know everything all at once, but knowledge and wisdom have their own rhythms. You must saturate yourself with knowledge as the slow water soaks into the fields. Then, yes, you will bear good fruit. Rushing knowledge passes through your mind too quickly. It will scarcely inform you and prove useless.

"Let us walk to the little stone bridge where we were this morning."

As we walked he told me, "This place is magical. The *capulí* trees, the running water, and this whole ambiance holds mystery. It attracts me very much, as it does your father.

"Besides, other beings, like nature spirits, accompany us, as you know. They listen to us. One may think very well in

69

peace and receive answers under those trees. For this to happen, you first have to pray and listen afterwards."

"What do you mean by praying and listening?" I thought.

"To pray is to ask Inti for what you wish. To listen is to wait for His answer. He always answers; you must know how to listen and to be permanently attentive."

"In other words, to pray is to ask God—to address Him. To meditate is to wait for a response. Is this it?" I asked.

"Yes, that is it," he answered.

"How interesting," I thought. *"The act of meditation has two parts—praying and meditation—namely to ask and to listen. The two attitudes go together, one after the other. I must learn exactly how to meditate before prayer."*

"This woodland has its charm. Always preserve it," he said.

"Of course, Amaru." I answered. "My father likes it very much. It is his favorite place; it speaks to him. We will keep it always."

He returned to the other subject. "What you call meditation is active and dynamic—not passive. There are many forms. It will depend on what you are searching for, but it is always dynamic. It is a mental process that permits you to understand or to clarify something. It is necessary to reflect and to concentrate oneself. It is thinking with discipline. As you say, the answer will come. It is putting yourself in contact with your Inti—the Inner One. The answer is nowhere else. Before beginning you have to be aware of your real self without pride. You are a being of light inside a physical body."

"I must become conscious of this reality. This is extremely important. If I cannot achieve this, I will not be able to function," I thought. It seemed very easy.

"Of course this is not easy. It also depends on your commitment," he answered. "You need to be humble and clear to know that you have a place in the universe—that you are part of the cosmos. Regard its beauty; admire it; give thanks to Life. Remember that Inti supports you permanently. Besides, there are beings of light in this universe who always accompany you.

"Begin by praying that this may become clear in your mind. Do not say the prayer but feel the prayer. It is an attitude. Do not speak or think any words. This state of mind is always primarily important. If you are tense, you need first to relax. You can become alert by doing some exercises such as dancing, jumping, or stretching your arms and legs. This not only helps you to limber yourself, but it also stirs your body's energies. When you feel it…"

"It comes like a little pleasant warmth," I thought.

"… it will be a signal that the time is propitious. Now, imagine that another body surrounds yours—outside your physical body, the etheric body. Envision it moving, dancing, balancing. Your physical body does not move itself. This other one moves your arms, your legs, and the rest of your body. Appreciate the difference. It is important to note that your physical body function on its own but depends upon this other body. Then, also imagine that you exit your body. Perhaps you stand if your body is sitting or you face yourself. Envision turning around, levitating, and seeing your spot from another perspective—say, from above."

How extraordinary! I was sitting beside Amaru with my feet dangling from the little stone bridge. When he said "stand up," I watched myself standing in front of me. Then, I elevated myself and saw my body seated next to Amaru. It frightened me, I abruptly fell and I immediately felt a headache.

"The best and only cure for fear is love. You do not have to comprehend anything. Always put a little warmth into it—your warmth—LOVE." He seemed a little vexed with my attitude.

I really had a fear of falling, and I *fell* in spite of the fact that this was not my first such experience.

He continued with much tolerance, "Imagine again that you are outside of your body—return gently, slowly, caressing yourself. Look at yourself; contract yourself; expand yourself; walk to and fro. Try to feel the changes. Now sing. Try to hear that sound inside you. What do you feel?"

"My body seems to be vibrating," I said.

"Now try to feel and see your organs. Examine your skin," he said.

"Yes! Even my cells vibrate with my tra-la-las. At least it seems that way to me." I said.

"Your whole body actually palpitates. It is visible, and you can get your tone by observing it. This is not an easy activity. You need to practice many times to find the proper tone, meaning the proper state of mind or state of being. Each of us has a tone. You need to search for it until you find it. Then your body will vibrate even more. This tra-la-la of yours is a chant, a mantra, that stimulates the important centers of your body up your spinal column. When this occurs, you begin to shine. You begin to move another very special energy that you have. You need to prepare yourself for this moment. Inside of the bones of your spine, in the medulla, the sciatic nerve branches into thousands of extensions that run through the entire physical body. This nerve has its energetic quality…"

"Does he mean the kundalini?" I wondered.

"…which is the philosopher's stone. All initiates have searched for this through the annals of time. Many people have coveted it; coveting is dangerous.

"I am going to show you some chants, some mantras."

He did this. I was very impressed. My body had goose bumps. One chant seemed to be a lament. Another sounded like a very firm command or a *pututo* [3] with its characteristic sound, but it was performed with the hands. There were various chants. Then Amaru asked me to imitate him. I tried. What I did was very different from what I heard him do!"

"Now you will practice," he said directing me to continue.

"As you see, this aspect of meditation is very stirring and dynamic. You can accomplish many things," he told me, enthused. "You can verify phenomena, improve yourself, and strengthen your convictions. You can also use colors—not for looking at, but for *breathing."*

"Breathe colors?" I asked.

"Yes, breathe colors," he repeated. "Imagine you can inhale colors to the top or to the bottom. To the top *seeing* as if there is a flow of light that runs over all of your body—from foot to head. Take for example the color of the second ray, about which our Master Nina Soncco already told you. Do you remember?"

"Yes I remember," I responded. *"At least I can remember this,"* I thought.

"I should hope so," he answered, with a mischievous look. "If you get good at this, your thoughts will become clear. It will give you wisdom. You have to breathe in very deeply to absorb colors from your feet. Everything depends on how you imagine it and how you *see* it. Now if you direct it from your head to the bottom, use the color of the fifth ray. You will notice that it has curative effects. It will calm you and give you peace. Learn and practice. Do not forget—alleviating illness is one of the most humanitarian acts."

In this moment, I understood why our concept of the cosmos is similar to that of the Orient. There are small differences peculiar to each place and era. This correlated to Amaru's teachings about the origin of man and languages: Quechua and Aymara are ultimately a single language.

"That is right." He looked at me. "There is only one knowledge. It arrived everywhere by different means. Then, our ancestors traveled and established those ideas at each site that they visited. They taught the natives from an approach that they could understand. Good, you are extracting what I want to teach you with your thoughts at each interval of time," he said to me offhandedly.

"Some colors appear cool, do they not? These serve to calm us. Warm colors serve to stimulate us. Imagine colors in the same way as I explained the spheres.

"Do you remember? I hope so. It would be incredible, if you did not remember, since it just happened," he continued smilingly. Take your mental picture of the spheres of creation. Now cover or fill them with color and light. Feel it, visualize it, smell it, and listen to it. If your imagination goes well, add sound. Breathe, give it movement, make it rotate, and walk over the rainbow."

While I listened to him, I imagined and *saw* what he described. How hushed my mind became!

"Of course, it gives you an inner peace and you do not enter into the mind game," he answered.

My thoughts are always chattering and do not give me much opportunity to concentrate.

"In this manner you keep it busy."

"This is very important because we also send orders to the subconscious. They remain there and flower when we need them," I thought. *"How interesting!"*

"That is right," he answered. He was reading my thoughts as usual. "Those orders and facts sink more deeply into the subconscious mind. Afterwards you can extract them as necessary. This is real; you can do it and with creativity. Really do it. You have to be precise in what you create with your mind and your thoughts. You move it; you give it life with your feelings. Each time you will come closer to Noccan Kani." He grew silent. He seemed to remember or see something.

He ordered, "Raise your arms. Do it."

I believed that he meant for me to do it mentally.

"Put yourself in the position in which you pray. Open your heart facing our Father Inti. Project yourself each time higher and higher to Him. He is the fountain of life. Look within— deeper—look. You are an Inti, radiant, vibrant, and full of light. You are near the very center of the universe—oh, this Black Inti that shines with its own Light. Be one with Him and then come back. RETURN and bring all of this experience to use faithfully without wavering. Indecision belongs to theories of knowledge without certainty... Now, compose yourself. Be calm."

I cried long and inconsolably. NEVER in life had I felt all of this realization. How could I not get excited? I was having a real experience. This was not fiction—this was a reality so significant that only I could know. I had known the theory. I had drawn the information, but I had NOT suspected the possibility of this experience. I had had quite a time these past few days! I could not say any one of them was more important than another.

I shouted with all of the air in my lungs, "Thank you my Father for giving me this opportunity—for the honor of having a master (in addition to the one who exists inside of this body who Amaru Cusiyupanqui calls I. A. Uma)! Thank you!" My heart pounded tremendously—like a drum. The beat sounded stronger each time.

The loving palm of his peaceful hands lay upon my breast. He spoke with great emotion:

"I know light. You are light. Be sure of this. You are inside a physical body and you are in the *beyond*. Feel yourself as you truly are. This is the only Reality. You can achieve many great things if you focus on it. Pray and you will feel how the response returns in meditation. You have to be here and you have to be there."

I opened my eyes. Amaru faced me with his hands on my chest. I looked at him. His eyes were misty with a very warm, loving look. In a moment a bright light grew from him and I could not look at him—he was radiating!

The afternoon was drawing to a close. The sunset allowed me to better appreciate the light shining from his eyes.

"Affirm," he said to me with a trembling voice.

I had not seen him like this before. He was still human.

"Trust completely in your experience and make your request. Father Inti will *descend* to your aid. You will be able to help others. You will be able to heal if you propose it. You can ask that all the people who suffer may find salvation. You can do this directly or from a distance without transgressing the laws. I will show you some techniques. Do not be afraid, do it. Visualize yourself in total harmony with the universe (of which you are a part). Your hands will be guided to do good. You have to convert yourself into His Hands.

Relive this last moment until it becomes part of you." He lifted his hands from my chest and gave me the hug of the *Ancient Ones*—very warm, very strong, firm, and very affectionate.

"Let us return home before Mamá comes calling us to eat. We can rest after dinner until morning."

We found my mother already looking for us on the road.

"Finally, I believe that you are learning that there is also an hour for meals," she said. "Good."

I did not want to argue with Mamá. I gave her a hug, and we all returned home. Amaru walked behind us. I still could not quiet my emotions. My mother saw this but said nothing.

My father was already seated and waiting for us. The sun of the third day had already gone down. The night slipped in too quietly as if it did not wish to shock anyone. Nobody seemed to be breathing; nothing was moving—not even a breeze, which we generally noticed by the gently waving light of the leaves on the trees. Today, nothing but the cold. Yes, the chill in the air allowed one to feel. The porch where we were sitting to eat had a kind of wooden balustrade without windows. My mother waited for everyone to be seated before she served hot dinner from the kitchen. She tempted us with a rich *laguita de moraya,* which was very spicy and delicious. It bolstered us. My father asked about Village A and Amaru's family.

"Everyone is very well. Chaska is already a married woman with children. Do you remember her?" he asked Father.

"Of course I remember. Does she still have those great black eyes and beautiful hair? She was a little girl the last time I saw her. How many children does she have?"

"Three." Amaru answered very proudly. "And the third one is a little boy who looks a great deal like Nina Huillca."

"Perhaps this is his reincarnation?" I asked.

"It is possible. He may have returned for some very special purpose.

"The eldest child is a girl. She looks a lot like Chaska and is very sweet. She always sticks to her father; she is constantly hugging and kissing him. The second one is also a girl. I believe she is the more serious of the two girls. She is an observer. She does not talk much and watches everyone. If someone new enters her hut, she studies them constantly, as if she would like to learn more about them."

"Perhaps she sees something more than usual," I commented.

Barely acknowledging me he continued, "Everything is at peace in the village. This is the dream era. The earth is resting. It absorbs energies to give life back in the spring and…"

"Did you say that the third one of your grandchildren looks like or is a reincarnation of Nina Huillca?" I broke in with a lot of interest. I had just realized something very important. I swallowed a big gulp of hot coffee and burned my mouth. "How could you know this? I had understood that you did not know the master of our dear Amaru Yupanqui Puma, right?"

"You did not have to burn your mouth to ask me this," he said smiling at me. "The coffee your mamá made is very pleasant. We should savor it slowly." He was teasing me. "It is always important to enjoy what we drink and eat to digest it properly. Food should not be bolted down as you just did."

"Yes, I burned my mouth," I replied trying to smile without feeling up to it. "It is just that I suddenly realized what you said. If you did not meet Nina Huillca, how did you know that your grandson looked like him?"

"You quickly forget our conversations or you are not paying attention. Then, you pressure me and put me on the spot with your questions." He was half joking and half serious at the same time. "I have to tell you again. Some truths are difficult for many people to comprehend. They do not remember, or they are never interested in investigating what happens beyond their physical eyes. There are other forms of vision. There is another way of seeing. We use this other sight to enter into the superior world and to learn about our

77

history. It is a kind of memory where everything is written down."

I believe that Amaru was referring to the Akashic Records or Nature's Memory.

"Nina Huillca was a great master; this is obvious by the masters he left us: Yupanqui Puma and Nina Soncco."

"Where do you fit in?" I thought.

"I am talking about Yupanqui Puma and Nina Soncco," he answered. This time, I believe, he felt irritated. "Before Nina Huillca came Ari Tambowacso, another master of the light. His name says it. In Runasimi, Ari is the word for light—the clarity that invades everything. It is like the air and that other something in the air we breath, that is, the ether. It penetrates everything. We cannot live without it. Ari was this way. They say that to be near him was to be reborn. He gave you life."

"I feel a lot of attraction to this person," I commented. "I love him."

"Soon we will talk about him," he said without further comment. "Tambowacso was prepared at that time by a woman named Urpi Killawamán. They say that she was an exceptional master."

"A female master?" I asked surprised.

"A woman has the same rights." He answered very seriously. "Inti is spirit; it makes no distinction between the female and male. I have to remind you that woman is the balancing element for man. She has other more important things to do other than being his companion in marriage and being a mother."

He left me speechless. I needed no other comment.

"My wife's parents rightly named her in memory of this great woman. They say of the first Urpi that ever since childhood she could perform extraordinary things. Besides curing with her hands and reading other people's thoughts, she predicted events and appeared in various places at the same time. She married a good man—a very hard worker, though not of her same spiritual development. Nevertheless, their relationship was excellent until he became

78

gravely ill and died. What irony! She was not able to do anything to save him; that is the law. By that time, her master Inti Wayna Koriwamán had already elected her as his successor. She was serving him according to the custom of the time, which has remained the same. We should never stop talking about the masters. Perhaps we will have another opportunity later.

"During the past few days, we have used several ways to mention *the return* , the reincarnation or rebirth—a new birth. This is renewal—the return of beings to physical life. Its purpose is to evolve. This may not always happen. We always commit indiscretions of free will. These injure our spiritual growth. We must serve in order to progress.

"A certain aspect of us is permanent and complete, it is individualized. It inhabits and animates the human body. When we die, that is to say when we leave this world, we pass to another body after a sabbatical in other *houses*, other planes or levels of existence. We return to this earth, or to another planet, where we fulfill our missions to overcome our weaknesses. We may receive help. Moreover, we may feel an affinity for the other beings who reincarnated with us and share the same goal. As you can see, we all return to the environment that is the most favorable for our level, quality, and vibratory frequency.

"The part of us that is Inti leaves the dense body. It passes to a higher *house* where it exits as a superphysical form of life for a while, in a world without time. Then, the Inti-self returns in another body to gather experience in a new existence. It is always seeking development.

"This natural phenomenon has nothing to do with religion. It happens whether we believe or not. Understanding it will bring us happiness and tranquillity when facing what we call death. It also helps us to understand why we are here, who we are, from whence we come, and to where we are going. Mankind has been asking these questions since we began our *return*. Time has passed, and our pride has prevented us from finding a proper understanding of this matter. We will need to know more about our lifetimes as we, with sincerity and humility, seek the answers and accept this law as a viable possibility. This increasing desire to obtain information will bear fruit."

He looked at me and asked, "Have you ever thought that each individual person can have a defined mission, or do you feel that this is possible only for a few?"

"I believe that everyone has a mission in life," I answered.

"What happens is that the majority of people are uninformed. They do not bother to investigate it. They do not even consider who they are. Consequently, they do not think that a mission is an important divine element in the universal plan of creation. They do not want to accept that the earth is the temporal stage for the drama that they voluntarily chose. They do not consider that at the end of their days they have merely finished one chapter of life and will have to excarnate from this earth to return later. Reincarnation to this same planet or to another one is not part of their thinking.

"As we see, there is an extended survival of the simple personality. This is the permanent, immortal person. Noccan Kani is very different from the human body. Death as we know it releases that invisible something. It soars to the greatest heights, to other planes of existence where neither time nor space exists. There it manifests itself because it is immortal without changes nor modifications. It continues to climb from *house* to *house,* according to its spiritual growth."

I tried to clarify what he had said. "Does this mean that there are many levels to which we must ascend according to our merits?"

"Do you believe that consummate growth," he interrogated me, "is achieved in only one *house?*"

"Of course not," I answered. "We must live this knowledge. We must overcome the most difficult times and continue forward in spite of the obstacles that we encounter hoping that some day we will shake free from the shackles that tie us to the ambition, egoism, and envy that are very pecu-

80

liar to our world. We will succeed at some time to ascend to the true life."

"I am glad that this is clear," he commented. "Many people claim to not believe in *the return*, but they say it without understanding this principle—without ever investigating it. It is understandable, then, that they do not accept it. What is not understood is not accepted. If popular opinion has misrepresented something, it is even further rejected."

"Of the millions of beings on earth, three quarters accept and believe in reincarnation. Those who believe it outnumber those who do not believe it," I thought.

"I am referring to our own people," he said. "The perspective is different beyond the great rivers and seas. The problem is created when there is intolerance, fanaticism, or ignorance. However, if we consider that our more cultured, scientific, religious brothers give credit to this principle, I believe that the least we can do is dedicate some minutes to reflect on this theme and to consider its likelihood."

"The popular critic," I quoted, "is not always the best to judge our convictions."

Amaru continued, "Be cautious also with that very enlightened and well known but fanatic associate. He presents an ignorant or deliberately slanted public perspective on this important and very beautiful natural law. He unjustly confuses other beings who listen and follow him. We cannot expect better from people who have not had the opportunity to acquire his knowledge. Their opinion will certainly be erroneous."

"How clearly Amaru explains his concepts—not to mention the warmth that he puts in it," I thought.

"This principle continues, as I told you. It is a natural law. It is not a religious credo, but it indeed has much to do with evolution. However, this is not religion either; it is within the plans of Inti."

"I understand. This is not religion but represents the divine principles that govern these processes. Is that so, Master?" I asked.

"This is so," he replied. "What must remain clear is that man is here living in a physical body, acquiring earthly experiences. We must take into consideration why or for what reason the questions exist. We will know and exactly understand the questions in our investigations of life in proportion to our interests. Inti does not allow anything to remain incomprehensible or unknown to us. He is shouting to us from within; we do not listen to Him. What a shame! Nevertheless, we can say publicly that this was impossible in the past. All the churches tell us that we are here because He created us to live on earth seeking evolution. Science also examines evolution, but up to this time it does not explain to us the finality of our existence—in spite of its honest search. Meanwhile, the absolute laws and principles continue to act and manifest themselves. They will continue whether we like it or not. We can live without fretting over these things. However, we will be happier if we understand these natural, divine laws that accompany our existence. Man is one and yet two (a dual unity). He has a physical body that is mortal. This is his apparent manifestation. He is a superior solar entity—immortal. Pleasure and pain, happiness and sadness, satisfaction and dissatisfaction, peace and suffering, love and antagonism, and all the other feelings find expression in his body. Inti is in the solar body, which IS. He demands the best for His manifestation. Between these two bodies develops the struggle to obtain the victory. Lamentably, the first one has a shield so thick that it does not allow that real presence to get through. Until now, the physical body has dominated and governed. Nevertheless, we do have knowledge that something very important and great exists within our body. It is not precisely physical and tangible but is very subtle and carries another type of divine consciousness."

"We all accept that man is dual," I said. "Science does not accept it but religions do. They consider an inner self or superior *I*, and an external self or inferior *I*. We hope that science will discover the inner. Then, it may realize that the human body is but the most external shell of something internal—of spiritual consciousness."

Amaru nodded and continued smiling. "Science and spirituality used to walk together in the investigation of nature. Our ancestors taught us that man is essentially a sun, a spirit, covered by a body, rather than a body that has a sun within. The mortal body might disintegrate at any moment. On the other hand, the sun leaves that body. It takes another, which it constructs from the elements that nature offers it in the mother's womb. This work begins from the moment of conception . The child is born after the required time and grows and then that body which was formed grows old and dies. Death is a transition which leaves a vestment behind that no longer serves; it is perishable and will not last. We separate from it in order to later take another body, which is also finite. The immortal and incorruptible entities that we are continue along the path of evolution or return to the Father."

"Spirit is that which leaves. And the soul?" I asked.

"It is necessary to consider how we view the Inti that we are aside from our human bodies. The covering, the soul, acquires the form of the body. There the personality takes root. Noccan Kani is Inti, spirit. That what is taking the form of man without being the body is different. This remains with the wrapping for a time. Afterwards it disappears, it disintegrates."

"Spirit and soul are different—it's clear," I thought.

"The soul and the spirit, as you call them, are effectively different," he said. "The spirit Inti does not have shape. It is a sun that shines within a very subtle garment which acquires the form of the physical body. The soul is where the desires and feelings are manifest—where we see, think, feel, act. Inti governs some attitudes, however. It is necessary to say that It is not always obeyed; the body with all of its defects usually decides for us. The personality dwells in the subtle layer. It is bonded well to the physical body, whose feelings and desires differ from those of the soul. You see, first comes the spirit—it builds the physical body. Then comes the soul—

83

it protects the first. Finally comes the dense body—which is what we see. This is another very long topic. Perhaps we can continue it at another time."

"Gladly. That way I have a chance to see you more often," I said enthusiastically.

"I did not say that we would see each other the way we do now. It is possible in another manner. The spirit has life—that is clear. However, the soul does not have its own life; it depends on the spirit. It is not the creator; it disappears a short time after we leave the body. Spirit is the only immortal part. If the personality did not obstruct it, the spirit would manifest itself as human wisdom."

"Look at all the progress we would make if this were possible," I thought.

"It is clear that it is possible," he replied. "We could access higher *houses* —the fourth dimension—if we were living from our real level, the third dimension, with humility. It becomes difficult when there is no humility."

"It is hard to truly know ourselves," I said. "We always aggrandize ourselves. All men say 'I am now prepared to receive this or that' and 'I deserve something better, but I am stuck here.' This is another form of insincerity and lack of humility. We forget that birth and knowledge do not make us good people by themselves. Our actions are what make us good or bad."

"I believe we have had enough for today," Amaru said. He gave thanks for the dinner, rose from his chair, and retired to rest.

I had already had too much. I felt giddy with too many beautiful experiences and massive doses of knowledge. I needed to be alone to reflect and assimilate it all. I wanted to assimilate the teachings that I had heard. I took leave of my parents and went to my room.

Lying on my bed, I tried to remember the discussions of the day. Amaru had once said, "He who knows is on the road of understanding. He who understands does not suffer but loves. He who loves is wise. Love achieves what other methods do not attain. If you love, you are loved."

How true—how simple this is! How difficult this love is in life. God is love—even though love is not God, we come tremendously close to Him. We must seek the kingdom of love—being a drop of light in a universe of darkness. When we understand that our birthright is eternal life, we will not have to return; we will have converted ourselves into the image and likeness of the Father. How ironic! We ignore our great secret—we do not have form but are in the form. The soul acquires one form to the next form. We commit the grave error of considering matter to be the great reality. Thus it is very important to differentiate between what is real and what is false. Our bodies are distinct from us. It is clear that what we love does not always coincide with what our body desires.

These are the initial concepts of a remote past that our Quechuan grandparents preserved by oral tradition. The first cosmic birth in America again returns to the Andes by the spiritual spiral of evolution. We must now prepare ourselves, in all of our *houses,* to receive this Great Center of Energy Power. Each day it grows greater and greater. We are near a second birth (so says our tradition) where the old knowledge and techniques of the masters will rise again. We will handle energy as it relates to matter so that we may evolve more rapidly.

The night advanced rapidly. Slowly, I was overtaken by my dreams.

The Fourth Day

The fourth day dawned very cold. I arose feeling sad but without any apparent reason. Of course! Indeed, there was a reason—a very important one. It was the last day that Amaru Cusiyupanqui would be with us. He was the indisputable Illac Uma—the teacher—the Wise One. He was so humble that no one knew who he was when he accompanied me to the Urubamba market [1] to shop for food. The Ancient Wise Ones—the true masters—are like this. They pass unobtrusively without calling attention to themselves. They do not brag about what they know. They do not compete with those who claim to be experts. [2]

Last night was a night of reflection, as the preceding nights had been. I cannot tell you whether I really slept or whether I stayed awake. I am certain that I had many visions. I seemed to be in the company of Yupanqui Puma, Nina Soncco, Ari Tambowacso, Nina Huillca, and Amaru Cusiyupanqui. I was listening to them. At times, one of them would speak to me, then the face of another would appear. Each of them taught me something—sadly, I cannot remember what they said. This always happens to me. The only thing that I remember is that they talked to me of Samana Wasi, among other important things. Seven years had elapsed since my second visit to Village A. There I had received many teachings from Nina Soncco. In those days, I had had many difficulties in making Samana Wasi a reality. I lacked a great deal of what I needed to carry it through. As a result, I had accomplished very little so far. I was worried and afraid of making mistakes, but I would correct myself as I went along. The idea is beautiful and it is possible to perfect it. Besides, I will continue to improve it.

I was not aware of the moment when Amaru entered my bedroom; my dreams preoccupied me. He stood in front of my bed and looked at me. I quickly arose and greeted him. It was six o'clock in the morning. He smiled and asked me in Quechua how I was, if I had slept well.

"Our mother tongue is so sweet," I thought.

"As I have told you, Runasimi is the mother of all the languages. It expresses the real feeling of a sentence with a great deal of warmth. It functions very well when you wish to say something very important. You can say a great deal with only a few words." Amaru said. "Today is the last day that I will be physically here to preach at you." He smiled. "We are going to talk a little before Mamá calls us for breakfast. She is starting to light the fire in the kitchen. [3] I will wait for you in the garden."

He left. I followed him quickly in the direction of the kitchen. I passed through the inner patio and washed myself in the stream that passed near there. I greeted my mother and continued towards the irrigation canal. I thrust myself in icy water and finished waking up (I was still half asleep). When I returned to the house, Amaru was observing and caressing the hydrangeas that my mother cultivated next to other beautiful flowers.

"The life that Inti left upon the earth," he said, "manifests itself with extraordinary beauty in everything. Wherever you may go, you will find His loving hand. This place of light, Samana Wasi, is not unique. It would be very egotistical to think that we have lovely places only here. When you visit other points of the planet—"

"Will this be possible?" I wondered.

"Indeed, pause a little. You will verify that everything that Inti made is beautiful—inside and outside of the earth. All of the universe thrills you with its loveliness. Giving thanks to the Father for this gift is the least we can do. This garden is very lovely and has life, is that not so?"

"Yes, of course, I see it." I said.

"What do you see?" he asked.

"Well…" He had me cornered. "The plants also have life," I said in order to escape.

"I thought you were *seeing,* the light that surrounds the flowers, their aura, vibrates. Everything vibrates likewise in the earth, air, water, and fire. There are very tiny beings that move in subtle dimensions where they live and reside, giving life. Nature is alive. It has intelligent forces that are not mechanical forces but tiny suns, spirits of nature."

"Of course," I thought.

The elementals show themselves in the invisible worlds. They are subhuman entities that move in the etheric or astral material. For example the gnomes, elves, dwarfs, and little people of the rocks live in and below the earth. They work among the rocks, trees, and flowers. They build their homes in caverns, mines, and ruined manors that they cover with vegetation. They are the guardians of hidden treasure. They manipulate the etheric energy to construct minerals, rocks, and precious stones. Neither iron nor gold would exist without them. Children up to seven years of age and natural clairvoyants can see them. They work on solid matter—even the bones in our bodies cannot mend without their help. Ether is the primary element of their bodies; they belong to the earth and are terrestrial. They age in a way that is very similar to ours.

What is this ether? Nature—or the physical world—also has an invisible and intangible world. Our physical senses have not achieved sensitivity to that frequency. Consequently, material science has not explored it. This is the etheric world—air, electricity, and other unexplainable energies. Although these things are not visible, science knows that they exist and can measure them. However, ether is not detectable. Nevertheless, there is a very subtle substance—the most subtle that science knows. The *Diccionario de la Lengua Española* states that science predicts a hypothetical medium of great subtlety and elasticity. It supposedly permeates space; light, electromagnetic waves, and other particles transmit across it.

From an esoteric viewpoint, ether is a reality that nourishes the body. To the practiced clairvoyant, it is as real as solids, liquids, and gases. All of the vital forces that give life to nature—

including man—come from ether. This ether has different compositions and corresponding names such as chemical ether, ether of life, and reflector ether. We are not going to deny that modern physical science has had marvelous successes. Every day, scientific tools and skills verify more and more of the *other field* of human investigation. These real events are not tangible but are nonetheless very real. The chemical ether absorbs and discharges; as do plants, animals, and man.

In the water live the undines, nymphs, mermaids, daughters, and goddesses of the sea. We find them in the rain. They work in a friendly manner in all of the liquids—even in the fluids of the human body. These beings are extremely beautiful. They are more delicate than the gnomes. Their bodies are primarily formed by the vital ether reserved for maintaining a species. They live extremely happy lives. They live in the most evolved sacred places and are interested in the plants and the flowers; they interact with female and male plants.

Salamanders belong to the kingdoms of fire. Everything that burns is under their jurisdiction. They appear as tiny tongues of flame. They like incense. Because of this they are found in sacred places where fire is part of the ceremonies. They cause eruptions and explosions; therefore they live below ground. The reflector ether is their primary body component. They are present when we remember the past and reflect on the memory of nature. However, no high-level memory, where recall is very clear, defined, and permanent, can happen through reflector ether. The memories and images are cloudy and vague without clarity or definition. This is a very important fact—many clairvoyants hold only to these images without knowing on what level they are reading or seeing. The same happens to mediums, psychometricians, and other paranormal workers. They assume that they have true information; what they really *see* is what the ether shows them. They do not *see* beyond the reflections. Because of this, many who claim to have seen their past lives are wrong; they jump to erroneous conclusions.

The sylphs—spirits of the air—are born of the wind. They are transparent and are mistaken for the blue of the sky. They are responsible for the great storms at sea, thunder, lightening, shafts of light, breezes, and hurricanes. One sees them as gleams of light. They move with great velocity. They are the communicators—especially of human thought, radio, television, telephone, and other message media. Besides this, they are the guardians of humanity. We all have a 'guardian angel' in the sylphs. The luminous ether is their principal body component. They are responsible for the warmth of the blood in higher animals and man. They are manifest in the senses, including smell, hearing, vision, and touch. In cold-blooded animals the ether is involved with circulation. Chlorophyll and the color of flowers depend on this ether as do all of the colors of nature.

In the era that approaches, in about three hundred years, the nature elementals will have an even greater importance. That will be the era of air conquest. Many very interesting discoveries will be realized.

I raised my head and my gaze found the eyes of Amaru. They were observing me, full of wisdom. He contemplated me in silence, guessing my thoughts. I had missed the moment when he had stopped talking. I had been so preoccupied that I had not been aware of my mental wanderings.

"Excuse me, Master," I said, most upset with myself. "I lead myself astray."

"You do not have to excuse yourself. I have also learned a great deal through your thoughts. You expanded upon what I have told you about the diminutive life that exists in nature and in all of us. You are quite familiar with these life-forms."

"You put it very well. I feel familiar with them but still do not know them. I have not yet *seen* them," I replied.

"You will do so soon, I am sure," he said smiling. "The science that will help you is advancing."

"Perhaps," I said, "it is not necessary to invent so many apparati and sophisticated instruments—although they undoubtedly permit astonishing discoveries? Would it not be better to develop *oneself* more as a researcher, to discover the secrets of nature? We all have special inner faculties. They certainly help us to shorten distances, to *see* better, and to listen in a different way. The occultists or esotericists—all seekers of Truth—use these faculties to great advantage."

"Yes, it is necessary to talk with researchers," Amaru said. "I believe that they are finally opening the doors. However, we must not disown the continuing advances of science. How wonderful it would be if a researcher were also an esotericist or occultist!"

"Yes, Master," I replied. "But many people are afraid of it or perhaps distrustful. Occultism and esoterism are practically synonymous. Both signify things that are hidden and internal—not exoteric, external, or public. That is why the occult or esoteric student studies the mysteries of nature to develop the latent psychic powers in man. I believe that many of us could fit within this category. There are copious seekers of Truth."

"Do not worry, soon they will understand," he replied without giving it greater importance.

"Come, eat what is getting cold." My mother appeared, leaving by the main door which faces the garden.

We returned to the porch that was our dining room. After greeting us, my father said something that surprised me.

"You were talking about the elementals?" he seemed to be seeking confirmation of his intuition.

"Yes, Papá," I said. "How do you know?'

"You need not ask this now," Amaru answered while sitting down. My father said nothing, and we began to eat breakfast in silence.

"Now, there is nothing to talk about in your minds. Are you mute?" my mother said with a very light smile on her lips.

The three of us replied with a smile.

"The reason is that the coffee is very delicious," said my father. "So are the bread and pastries." Amaru and I agreed nodding our heads. Everything was in fact very pleasing, but I believe that what had silenced us was the proximity of Amaru's departure. None of us wanted to touch this subject.

Plate 5

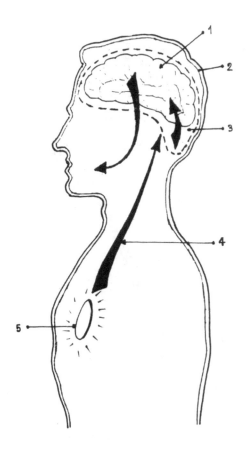

1.BRAIN
2.SOUL
3.CONSCIOUSNESS
4.PATH BY WHICH ORDERS FROM THE SPIRIT TRAVEL
5.SPIRIT

Plate 6

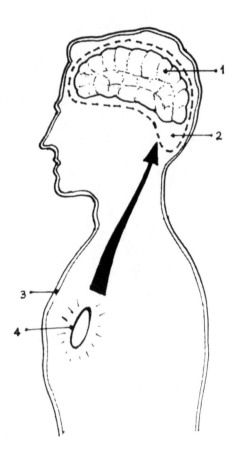

1.BRAIN
2.CONSCIOUSNESS
3.SOUL
4.SPIRIT

Plate 7

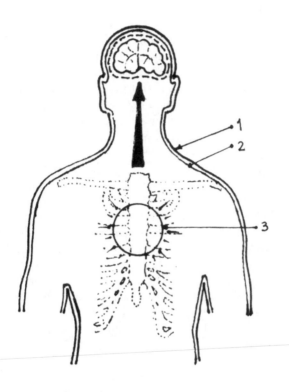

1.PHYSICAL BODY
2.SOUL
3.SPIRIT

My father and I (especially I) would feel his absence very much.

"There is no absence." Amaru said very seriously. "Our minds will always communicate and be busy with memories, with the teachings, with the experiences, and with responsibilities—if we learn to train our thoughts."

"How do we do this?" I asked.

"The mind and the consciousness are in the soul and not in the spirit {Plate 5}. We have said that the soul and the spirit are not the same. Can we also say that the soul is consciousness and the spirit—or Inti—is Life? The true Life? Inti sends an order in the form of thought to the mind {Plate 6}. The mind sends this information to the brain, which processes it well or poorly {Plate 7}. It manifests itself and shows up in the body by word or by attitude.

"Consciousness is incorporeal and individual. As you will come to understand, consciousness is not the product of the body, nor does it depend on the body for existence. It exists through Inti, which is Life. The body does not do anything by itself. For example, consider a cadaver. The body of a living person owes its functioning precisely to the soul and fundamentally to Inti. If you—like the sun that you are—learn to train the mind perfectly, your body will not have problems of any kind and will always be well. The mind determines the well-being or discomfort of the body. Therefore, training the mind is very important, because your commands will be obeyed. If you wish to live in illness, then ill you shall be. On the other hand, if you wish to live a healthy and strong life, your attitude must be absolutely positive and firm. The life that you live depends only on the orders from your mind to your body."

I broke in, "Does this mean that physical symptoms are manifestations of psychic conflicts?"

"That is correct," Amaru answered.

"This is the way to discover a patient's problem," declared my father. Normally, my father never spoke up!

Amaru looked at him with sympathy and continued his dissertation. "The symptom is only an external effect. It is necessary to enter the interior to undo the *mental cause.* Struggling against the external effect only limits us. It is like cutting a weed instead of pulling it up by the roots. One must work energetically to remove the compulsion—to smoke, to drink alcohol, or to eliminate a headache—until one is successful in to eradicating the torment or the cause. Then the external effect will also end. Mental patterns—criticism, envy, rage, guilt, and resentment—cause the majority of the body's diseases. We must first extinguish the mental cause; we will thus forever prevent the problem. No plant lives if we pull it out by the root. We have to be entirely responsible for our own health—we have to love ourselves. The lack of love for our own selves is the origin of many diseases. We must accept ourselves[4] as we are—here and now. When we understand this, the energy that we wasted for such a long time—through misunderstanding to desperation—will become dedicated to curing and healing our bodies from our own instigation. Loving our own selves frees us from everything, soothing any discomforts we may feel. Discomfort originates from nothingness; it returns to nothingness. We must strive to find and maintain the equilibrium of the body and mind and spirit. This is a positive action for ourselves and for life in general. We will feel the joy of living when we achieve this harmony. It depends on us—on no one else."

"What happened to you?" my mother commented entering the porch where we ate breakfast. My father and I stared at Amaru. Our eyes were growing wider.

"What topic could turn you into statues?"

The three of us laughed.

"I am going to bring something hot. This must be frozen by now." Having said this, she returned to the kitchen.

This interruption effectively broke the intensity of the mood. Everything was so interesting and important! I believe that, to date, no researcher has succeeded in penetrating the secret convolutions of the Quechua soul. No one else has certainly had my opportunities. The very system is self-contained to nurture, protect, and defend its sublime and sacred cultural values from all the invasions that Perú has suffered. This explains the prevalent ignorance of the past—and perhaps of the present—spiritual reality that pulsates in its tradition, in our tradition.

My father said, "Men have made up a cultural entity as a historical process. This is not our natural reality."

Surely he was also picking up my own thoughts.

"This mythical material, both old and young, will be interpreted only if we penetrate ourselves deeply and intimately in the manner of our Quechua ancestors' mode of thinking— of feeling and of expressing. We need to explore the most profound layers of their thinking, their mental processes and their religious ideas, as well as their spiritual reality. Then we would no longer view it as a fiction, a novel or fantasy."

Father gave me a meaningful look. "For you and for me, this is a reality that we are experiencing in different times…"

He became emotional and quiet for a moment. Tears welled in his eyes. His state was very contagious, at least for me. Amaru remained serene; I hope to learn this serenity someday.

Father continued, "Myths are historical narrations at the same time—that is to say mythohistorical. People do not wish to understand or accept them as facts. They are the fundamentals of cultural consciousness and are constantly living with their past; the past continues into the present."

"Don't forget," Amaru interrupted, "the present time begins with the third creation. The former age is older, prehistorical. The present is thus an accumulation of the past."

"The whole of history produces the present culture," my father quipped.

He continued to surprise me with interjections.

"Be very careful about this," he said looking at me.

I could not overcome my astonishment!

"Our village still has not become properly conscious of our heritage. Because of this it has not awakened from its long lethargy. We still have a great historical culture. Why have we made no use of it up to now? Our past is great; our present must also be great. This is the responsibility facing humanity. The present originates in the events of mythohistory. What is history? Isn't it mankind across time and space? Man develops into his manifestation as a social being. The Runasimi wrote the true history—the spiritual reality lived by their people—not just chronological events that have no value for the future."

Incredible! This was my father talking! I wanted to stand up—hug him—kiss him. But I dared not interrupt him.

"The Andean is the Runasimi—a model of man with history. So say the students of myth."

"How sad, there are so few of them," I thought.

"At present, this is not considered a scholarly pursuit. It falls into the field of science. A conceptual analysis will show the spirituality of the native, if we penetrate into the mental processes that are so different and distant from common man. Even so, we would fail to capture what is true in his life. To do this, we would have to live with the native in his own temples. Of course, these are sacred places hidden in the high mountains where development comes to life through oral tradition from the wisdom of ancient illiterate sages."

"Such as Village A," I thought.

Amaru looked at me and gestured that I should 'silence' myself.

Father continued without missing a beat. "Ancestral wisdom does not need our culture. In mythology, everything is history. Mythohistory explains an established truth free from hypothesis. It is a world unknown until now. The disciples of the entire earth, particularly those of the Orient, feel beckoned to South America—to the Andes mountains. As we know, here is one of the three apexes of energy. These apexes are responsible for the future of the planet and the New Age focus of illumination.

"Well, enough of this. Amaru can explain it with more knowledge and wisdom than I."

"Our beloved masters," said Amaru with solemnity, "have given us an order. We must establish houses or meeting places somewhere[5] more or less in the vicinity of the central retreats. These may have a special spirituality. The sincere and deliberate man and woman can receive knowledge to help improve through the act of service. He can return to the central retreat—to Inti Wasi.[6] It will be important to show him the way."

"Does he mean to initiate him?" I wondered.

"Yes, exactly that—to initiate him. The physical initiation will come through his giving service to others. The other, the psychic initiation, comes through knowledge; the spiritual initiation comes with wisdom which is knowledge converted to wisdom."

My mother interrupted us. "Well then, this has cooled off again." She seemed a little bothered. She had her quirks.

We had not noticed the moment that she had returned from the kitchen. We thanked her for her attention and concern. Then we got up from the table. I hugged my father and gave him a kiss. It was not necessary to say more.

Amaru left the house and went to the site of the future Samana Wasi.[7] I trailed behind him. He sat down on the little stone bridge with his feet dangling over the stream and I sat down beside him.

"These days we have talked about various important subjects. Your father also participated. I asked him to do it so that you would know who he is."

"Within the Brotherhood of the Sons of the Sun?" I wondered.

"Why has he not shared what he knows? Why must he continue to teach[8] in his assured silent loyalty? You have a great deal to learn from him."

I also knew my father's loyalty and responsibility concerning the Solar Brotherhood. I learned this with pain and shame, since I held a bad opinion of him for many years.

Amaru told me about my father. Clearly, I had not known him and was filled with emotion.

"Don't dwell on your mistakes. I believe that you understood perfectly," he said. "It suits you to do the opposite of your father, seasoned with much prudence and fair judgment. You have to talk with people and to explain what you know, even though they may not believe you. On the contrary they may prejudge you or treat you falsely. Some people's attempts to discredit you will simply be disguised envy. You have to prepare for this."

"Yes Master. I am sorry, but I am not worried," I said. "What does disturb me is that I don't know how to speak in public. How do I begin a conversation about these themes? Do I initiate it or do I wait? I do not know."

"Wait, always wait. Soon you will have the opportunity to do it when you publish your first book. Then you will begin. The contention will also be present immediately; do not pay any attention to it. However be alert to vanity. It is a companion that walks very nearby. It waits for a minor carelessness in order to pounce and to empower itself."

"It will be a danger for us. I do not believe that you will be susceptible," I thought.

He regarded me with his brows knitted. "All of us always have this danger of narcissism nearby. We must be watchful. We have to be aware of its possibility in order to overcome it. Do not relax for a moment against it. It would be a sign of weakness. An arrogant person 'openly closed' his eyes. His pride does not permit him to see. He goes to and fro, turning and turning."

"Like a carousel," I mused.

"Yes, like a carousel he never goes anywhere."

What clear examples he gave me. They simplified the concepts. These masters are all the same. It is as if they were a Pleiades of sages.

His dark, brilliant eyes looked at me lovingly. They seemed to be two stars in full morning.

"It is not necessary to hide or disguise the truth; all of us would lose then. It is important to be discerning about with whom you share it. The human condition is in a descent as never before. It has been degrading for a while." he looked worried. "Medicine has achieved many advances. However

101

in the schools—in high school and even in the universities—one sees a tremendous lowering of standards in order to gain more students. Yes, multitudes of poorly prepared children and young people with insufficient mental development are in the classrooms. The schools should always maintain their standards for enrollment—preferably they should raise them. A healthy society moves towards progress and triumph, rather than slipping backwards. In addition, some parents support their children's negative attitudes. These adults deceive and justify themselves with disguised ideas. They have no desire to see their terrible social sickness.

"This is not the fault of Inti or of natural disasters. We have generated this limited and sad future that we intend to ignore. Now listen. We are the only ones who can change these conditions, improve them in the conscious use of our free will. Remember that the best sermon is immediate action after the word. Use wisdom correctly with works of love. Help a neighbor with generosity. I still have various things to speak to you about. Time is short, so pay attention to me. You must think, reflect, and meditate in order to get to *work.*

"The initiation of which we have spoken is a sacred and preparatory ceremony for another, greater one—the true initiation. The names are not important. One follows the other. The prospective initiate, he who seeks, is always perfectly conscious of what he wants.

"Metaphorically speaking, the seed is planted in a good furrow—rich and fertile with the *guano*[9] of high values, ethics, and profound love. The seed will germinate and sprout up a firm and strong seedling. Nothing will divert it from its path. It will be prepared to resist all temptations. It will immediately start radiating its warmth and its knowledge to the rest. This warmth will be like a fire. When it is burning, it heats first the hearth and then spreads its warmth all around.

"This initiation will imbue the first impulse. The second initiation will soon follow on its own merits. It will depend entirely on the work that develops. It is important to include every honest seeker who can take advantage of it for his growth. Otherwise, it would be quite a pity to miss the opportunity. The proselyte will have to adjust his attitude about life in order to deflect his own thoughts, the thoughts that have caused most of his problems. If he achieves this, he will always be in the Light. He will fear nothing. He will speak truth and think truth that is love. Truth is not just speaking the truth, it is living the truth. It is working in life with rectitude and humility, a virtue that will bring him close to wisdom. A Wise One is like a bough laden down with fruit—he is bent with humility by the weight of the wisdom. We should all aspire to this precious treasure of character.

"What do you think?"

"Nothing. You told me not to think while you are talking," I replied.

He smiled and said, "Now I am asking you."

"Well," I said, "I am working in order to be able to begin the work—Samana Wasi. As you know, my father donated all of his land to serve the homeless children and elderly. We will dedicate this and our lives to serve them. We will also serve the Brotherhood with much love, into which I have had the great honor of you initiating me."

"I did not initiate you," he said surprised. "It was the Illac Uma Nina Soncco. I only helped to—"

"You showed me how to walk," I interjected.

"And how do you know it was I?" he asked.

"Ah! I also see sometimes—or I sense what is happening!" I laughed.

He looked at me mischievously and smiled. Then he said, "Service helps the server. It is a very great virtue that gratifies the giver, but watch out—you must be objective."

"Of course," I answered him, "this is clear."

"Education without love is not good; take this into consideration. Besides, for influence to be constructive, the one who sets the example must live with the child. If a new type of man is to emerge from Samana Wasi, he will have to be a higher form of *being.*"

"A man better than man?" I asked.

"Of course," he responded. "It seems that you still have not correctly understood the direction of the future. Evolution continues; it does not stop. We are pursuing the path to super-man. This new being will be completely conscious of his faculties and possibilities, besides being clairvoyant. He will be an elevated life form. This must succeed. Do not be afraid. You will always have our help."

"Thank you Master, but I am not afraid. I am terrified."

He smiled and continued, "The more you serve, the more you grow in every sense. You expand yourself. There are people who continue believing in pretense; they are mistaken. Their achievements deteriorate quickly. In order to survive, it is necessary to have heart, to have spirit, and to be desirous of giving. This is not wasted. However I repeat, be very careful with pride, vanity, and arrogance. Material or intellectual gains can give you knowledge and comfort but no wisdom."

"All of this has become clearer," I said. "I will be very careful. I now know that these vices are very close companions. They push us to commit mistakes. They inflate our egos and cause us to believe that in this way we are elevating ourselves. What stupidity! Thank you, dear Amaru, for reminding me of it."

"Let's move on to another topic," he continued.

"You must exercise the faculties that will help you to evolve and serve efficiently. We know many people who say 'love your own children.' They believe that these young people are their property. This is not the case with you now. Those other adults feel indifferent to anyone not tied to them by kin. Not only is it necessary to love your own children but all the children of earth. You will have to learn this, because you will have many children."

"This is so," I agreed.

"The only authentic and true relationship between men is friendship. It is the greatest tie. All relationships fail when this does not exist. When it is present, all relationships grow constructively. Lamentably, we seldom find it in our civilization. Ambition and self-interest are destroying almost all of the beautiful feelings. You will soon experience this disillusionment first hand, when you renounce your present career to dedicate your life to Samana Wasi."

"I hope that it will not be too stressful," I thought.

"I also hope that it will not affect you," he answered and continued. "The love for home and devotion to our birthplaces or where we live—for the special places that bring us pleasing memories of infancy, youth, and relationships—are very important. We learn to love all of earth. The entire planet is our homeland. To defend and to respect your home is to defend and respect the great home without losing individuality. All creation is a manifestation of love—love that makes us free. The man who gains his liberation is totally unique—even in his physical body, temperament, and expression. That love is the only cure for fear. Fear prevents us from confronting reality. You will never understand a theoretical piece of knowledge if you did not experience it directly. Experience is not found in books."

"Of course not," I said. "However, I can find it when my master grants me the honor of teaching me directly."

He ignored me and continued his thought.

"You have to persist in what you start until you complete it. We do not generally use this strength. We begin various things but we finish very few. Because of this, one does not feel good, one is frustrated. Your vitality depends on finishing everything you begin. If you do not, life on earth will be very short. Your character has to be strong and firm but with sweetness to lead justly and prudently. Respect yourself. This will give you confidence, faith, and stability (sureness in your intentions). You must learn to be just, honest, and virtuous—with a sense of responsibility to others. You must always hope that today's dreams will come true tomorrow. Faith in Inti will give you perpetual stability. His presence will shine through all that you do—loving the ancient traditions, respecting those who are superior or old and serving them, being amiable, helping the needy, and distributing what you have."

"I do not know what I have to distribute," I thought.

"Do not be surprised when Inti provides you with things to distribute among the needy children and elderly. Imitate the good examples that you find. Accept them with humility. Try to understand others. With sympathy, try to help them through the difficult times of life, gently without overpowering. Respect the time of other persons and do not tire them with empty chatter. When you speak, always give something. We both know people who visit us for five minutes and stay all day."

We laughed.

"There are millions everywhere," he indicated. "Make sure that your words are always harmonious like your private and public life, the language must be adequate and must not wound. Beauty is in everything and in everyone. You have to recognize it, and that is good. Always take into account that the law of cause and effect is manifest. It will help you at times to draw the invisible cause from the visible effect. At the same time, do all this with a sense of humor."

"I must be cheerful," I thought.

"That is right. Humor is one of the greatest friends of man. Practice it."

Amaru suddenly changed the subject. "From this moment on you will also be able to think without using your mind."

"How?" I exclaimed.

"Do not be frightened. What will happen is that you will have the power of my mind supporting you. It will be at your disposal. You will be able to think with my mind and not with yours. In this way you will receive more knowledge. This will save me time so that I won't have to come here. There will be times when you will transcend yourself. You will not be able to

106

explain how you came to know something. Do you understand?"

"I—believe—so," I stammered. "In reality I will always have my own thoughts but with the advantage that I will also be able to use the power of your mind?"

"They have authorized me to do this," he said. "You will leave 'like a shot' from your body to find what you are seeking. You will probably not even notice doing this. It does not matter. We will be supporting and watching over you. We will safeguard all of your labor for the children and elderly. From now on we will also be at your side spiritually."

I firmly embraced him with much emotion and gratitude.

"Let us stop, because right now Mamá is coming to call us. It is time for lunch," he said while standing up.

"It is not because your stomach is empty?" I said joking.

Mamá's energetic voice punctuated the air.

"Come to lunch. The plates are now on the table and if you do not come quickly, they are going to get cold."

Amaru always had a premonition before she found us.

My father was already waiting seated at the table. He rubbed his hands together to warm them. The day was cold in every way, although I had not felt it. The sun had been out all morning, and I was very busy listening to my dear master.

"Amaru, what time are you leaving? I want to prepare something for you," Mother said.

"Thank you. I will be going well at the break of dawn tomorrow," he replied.

"Wonderful!" I said. "We still have the whole afternoon ahead of us to enjoy your company."

"After lunch we will rest. Then we will meet again at the stream. You may get used to being there," Amaru laughed.

"Besides, we have to magnetize that place with a lot of power so that the energy can grow everyday. It is already special. Its legendary name is *Almacunayoc* or *Animasniyoc*. These words are a mixture of Quechua and

Castilian, but the important thing is what is behind the name. It acquires value because of this.

"It is the same when we look at a thermometer—yes, exactly this. The mercury rises through the tube and it has no greater significance to us. However, if we know that this climb is marking the temperature, it takes on a meaning. In the same way, the importance of our body is established because we are within Inti. Isn't this true?"

"Yes, of course," I said.

Father commented, "When people stop interpreting what happens around them or to them, they deteriorate into incoherence and absurdity. What is needed then is a frame of reference. This frame is outside of what one needs to know."

"Because of this, everything in this material world of form will be interpreted in the beyond," Amaru said.

"Do you mean like a metaphysical reference?" I asked.

"Yes," my father agreed. "In time, the visible world of form changes into allegories. In the same way, letters and numbers form abstractions of an underlying idea. Everything visible is an expression of an idea. Therefore, it is the intermediary to what is invisible—the form and its content."

"This is becoming interesting," I thought.

My father continued, "The content that gives meaning to the form is manifested in the form. Because of this, letters— which do not carry ideas or something significant—remain senseless and empty. When you speak, always give something constructive that helps—not destroys. "

"Yes, Papá, I will always try to do so," I replied.

"Thoughts give form to our lives," Amaru said. "If we desire to lead a successful life, we have to think meaningful thoughts. Everything we send out—mentally or verbally— will return to us in the same form. Nobody thinks in your mind but you."

"Of course, of course," I said joking. "You two have it in for me.

"No son," my father said. "We are reflecting aloud about

something so important that it also touches me. Both of us are benefiting."

"All three of us," corrected Amaru. "We are beginning. The most insignificant beginning is already important. Inti alone can judge us with true greatness; He knows the heart of man."

"This will happen when we excarnate. Why?" I said.

My father spoke. "To be born and to die are not different, but—yes—different aspects of the same state. Life is one. It is there where our Father will judge us."

"It is necessary to live life happily," I commented.

"Yes, if you know the appropriate way to live," Amaru said. "Life is creativity. It is a permanent creation. It is necessary to fulfill it in order to be happy. We have come with all assuredness to be happy, and we *must* be so. The reality of life is not simply material or exclusively spiritual. However, one cannot seek wealth and at the same time pretend to be at Inti's side. Is that clear—as you would say?"

"Yes Master, it is clear," I said with enthusiasm. "One needs to keep one's feet on the ground—not accumulate riches but live spiritually—balanced without worldly attachment."

Amaru laughed and said to me, "But don't forget to dig well into the earth and plant the seed correctly. If you forget this, it is like forgetting yourself."

We finished lunch and went to rest.

Reclined on my bed, I remembered all the minute details of the morning and of lunch. Father and Amaru had truly given me a great deal of knowledge—living knowledge. The time was coming to put it into practice. It was my hour. Would I be able to succeed? I thought so. I understood that there would be difficulties. Life on earth is a school in which we learn any way we can, experience that is important for our growth. Much will depend on how we pass this test. I am worried, but each day I feel more sure about everything. I have the support of my father and of my *elder brothers*. How lucky I was! If it were not for my father, I would be still searching and would continue searching until who knows when.

"I believe that you have rested enough, although I bet you have been thinking and not resting."

Amaru startled me as usual, appearing without any preamble.

"Let's go. We only have a few hours left." He left my room and went toward the future Samana Wasi. I followed him immediately. I could not afford to lose this opportunity. These days had been more than happy. They had all been times of learning.

We sat again on the little stone bridge. He really liked this place. His feet hung over the stream and touched the water. I could not reach it. He was tall and very slender.

"The water is the path," he said. "It is always necessary to be in contact with it, as with other elements. Loving and respecting them brings us close to Inti."

"Was the solar disc found in the *Korikancha*[10]?" I asked.

"Yes and no," he replied. "Two solar discs of gold were in the Korikancha. One was brought out for public ceremonies. The other one was even more sacred than the first; it was only used in transcendental times or occasions of cosmic character. It came from very far across the great river behind these mountains, from Lemuria." Amaru motioned westward to the Pacific Ocean. The great masters of these lands are our very distant ancestors."

"How?" I said.

Again, he had astonished me. To listen to this master was truly a very great and important honor. Time with him was full of fabulous, incredible adventures.

"This and other knowledge will undoubtedly surprise you even more. I do not know if we will speak about anything else. I believe we may have another chance for this. From this day on—as I told you this morning—we will always be in contact. Each time that you have doubts, call me. I will be *present*. Who knows? Not like this but—yes—you will hear me," spoke Amaru. "I told you before that the Andes cradled thousands of cultures—that is to say the region where the Andes are now. Modern science is right sometimes. Geology teaches us that the 'new world', the Americas, is older than the 'old world', Eurasia. Look at our language. It is extremely ancient. Its very antiquity can fix the place of the first man. The culture of a nation is related to its language; our culture was truly great."

My mouth dropped open. It was clear that he knew what he was saying.

"Listen," he said to me, "the great masters knew that their land would be deluged. They were in contact with their forefathers—with their Andean origin (we will call it this for now). They decided to officially send their people. At the head of this transcendental delegation they appointed a mystic—it could not be anyone else such as an apostle or reformer. Now do you understand me a little better?" he smiled.

"Yes Master, I hear you and understand," I answered with nervousness. I had good reason.

"They considered this mystic to be almost the same as Inti," he continued.

"The god Merú," I thought.

"Yes, this one. Well, from now on I am not going to answer you when you think, except when you are wrong. You keep interrupting me."

I nodded with my head and mentally said to him, *"Why then do you read my thoughts? I didn't ask you to do so?"*

"Of course you have not asked me, but you are thinking so strongly that you may as well be shouting in my ear," the Master replied. "Let us continue. This Inti was known by his followers by a different name—Aramu Muru. He came with his wife Arama Mara. We welcomed them here when they left the Sacred Lake, Lake Titicaca, as Manco Ccapac and his wife—"

"Mama Ocllo," I said, interrupting him again.

"Mama Ocllo, it does not mean anything," he answered. "Don't you believe it is more correct than Mama Aclla?"

"It could be," I said.

"The rest is common knowledge. It came to us as a legend. This is our tradition, even though it has slightly changed. He was our supreme chief. He carried a staff and wore tassels, sashes, belts, and other adornments—all in rainbow colors. [11] To the physical eye it was impressive, and more even so when you *saw* his wisdom. Both, Manco Ccapac and Mama Aclla wore bright yellow gilding to symbolize the sun. With them came the Ccapac Cuna, bearers of the *mascaipacha*. This all happened before the time of the Inca. Regrettably, our tradition does not preserve this. Perhaps the gaps in our recorded history are due to the dark ages, similar to Medieval Europe. Although we are speaking of a very ancient time, we do know about it. Without tradition there is no native homeland. We have to preserve it and make it known.

"Metaphorically speaking, when the bar of gold sank in Huanacaure, the initiates began special rites. *Huanacaure* means God of the Storm, symbolizing meteorological activity. The storm changed and the calm returned with more pure and clear air. The ceremonies helped the process of change and purification. From then on and by all the genuinely spiritual work they did, *El Quosqo* [12] was declared a sacred place. From then on, we made pilgrimages to Quosqo. We held the Sacred City's old age in the highest respect, with devotion to its temples and special past. All of us—both natives and strangers—come as pilgrims, as they do in other places of the earth, Mecca, for example. We seek the spirituality and the sacred footsteps and purifiers of our past. There we will find not only our Inca infancy but the furthest of our Andean past. When we speak of Quosqo, we do not merely refer to the Inca—they are of the present—but to our history."

He was silent. I watched him. He seemed very emotional and sad.

Our national identity urgently needed to recover itself in order to achieve decolonization. The *mestizaje*, i.e., the crossing of Spanish and Indian races, is irreversible in Indian America. It has not blended into a *mestizaje* culture because

112

the groups in power—the *criollos*, the descendants of the Europeans, have not permitted it.

"You are showing yourself as an Indian, now," he said more tranquilly. "The second solar disc was the symbolic representation of the Inti, the Great Central Sun. The Andean square cross represents the Great Regulator of cosmic energy—the apostle and reformer Manco Ccapac. At that time, only he knew how to manage the great energy and how to direct it. He restored the lost knowledge. Lamentably, there are times of obscurity in our history. Because of this, we do not remember all of the past epochs.

"The Sacred Lake Titicaca, Tiwanacu, Cuzco, and Machu Picchu are sacred centers. They are temples where we find the true history of humanity. The people who visit these places should remove their shoes as a sign of respect and humility. Does it seem awkward that I say this?"

"No, Amaru, it does not seem awkward to me, " I answered. "However, people will have some difficulty in truly understanding the value of these four places."

"When they meditate, this truth will enter their minds with clarity, and it will convert into an attitude. People take off their shoes in order to enter their temples and sacred places elsewhere in the world. Soon, you will see. You will have to remove your shoes, too."

I said, "From now on, Master, if I have the opportunity, I will do so with much respect. The presence of God is in all of the temples of different religions. The only thing that changes is the name they give Him."

"Yes, this is also true in brotherhoods where people join in order to learn. Lastly, Inti is everywhere," he said. "In the *ayllus* we used to come together at a certain time in the day to pray. [13] Today nobody remembers this. The *ayllu* is an organization much more ancient than the Inca. When we speak of our past, it seems that we only refer to the Inca. Our history is pre-Inca. Soon it will be revealed. The history that we learn in school these days is merely the repetition of copycat civilizations. They even copied the ceremonies that we see. These days, the person who performs ceremonies arranges them to suit his personal taste. Written history up to now is that of the Spaniards in America; it has not included our native histories."

"This is true," I said. "The name America—as I understand it—did not come from Amergo Vespucci. It derives from another word that means 'land of the immortals'. *Amara* means 'immortal god', and *Ka* is the name for land. Therefore the name America comes from *Amáraka.*"

"The name comes from Runasimi," he said with confidence. "America has always been called America. It was known all over the world. The title Amaru also derives from this word. America also means 'where Inti the Lord of the Sky reigns.'

"We have digressed a little from what we were saying," he said. "The men and women of the future will not think it ridiculous to remove their shoes when they enter Korikancha, Tiwanacu, and Machu Picchu. It will seem stupid to them that we have lived down the centuries as an isolated nation separated by borders. A new religion will unite all humans of earth through the current philosophies. No single person has solved the great riddle of the origins of our planet, our solar system, other worlds farther away, or the genesis of man on Earth. We are thus living with many enigmas. In the universe there are many planes and places inhabited by conscious beings. This is true even though we may have difficulty understanding it."

"Spheres of evolution are like bubbles of light that do not change," I thought. The Master looked at me.

"Inti is the Father who does not change. Everything that He does is forever. To you, He might seem mutable because of your evolving human nature. Inti's plan is eternal. It does not change because it is perfect and constant. It is beyond time and space. He has created the universe of universes. Everything is His creation. What is imperfect is our own personality. However, He even shares this imperfection of ours; he gives us the possibility to evolve on the spheres of

114

His creation in the different universes. *Noccan Kani* is the key and *Paima Kani* is the culmination of this way. Eventually, we will perfectly learn all about creation and evolution. Inti lives on and within each body. He will guide us—when we become aware of this knowledge—forever, step by step, life after life, in each *return*, reincarnation, from sphere to sphere of creation, to the end—to Him who is within us helping us to arrive.

"Each short excursion that we take into physical life is a cycle of reincarnation. This is not a religious belief, neither a doctrine nor religious law. It is a natural law related to the evolution of nature. In this epoch, we hear many marvelous words spoken by people who do not live what they say. They must integrate this knowledge with their daily activities so that it serves them first. Thus they unexpectedly change for the better.

"The birth of a new universal consciousness is important for several reasons. We will become more united. We will learn to share without losing individuality. We will completely respect nature. We will spiritually grow in harmony. War, poverty, and injustice will disappear. We will finally be able to live the *Noccan Kani* —our true identity.

"This will empower us to come more closely to Inti and serve Him better. Remember that service can advance the payment of our debts to accelerate the karmic cycles. Perhaps what I tell you may serve as incentive for a few people to reflect and change. Then they will begin to see the neighbor as a brother. This brotherhood is stronger than blood ties, religious and scientific dogmas, or flags and borders. These latter things have only served to separate and divide men.

"We said that it is necessary to share life without fear or egoism so that life will not seem hollow. We are always striving to be good; at other times we make mistakes. However, we can discover *Noccan Kani*—which is the true identity—by remaining balanced and attentive, and by walking with a firm, slow, consistent step. You will come closer to Inti. You will understand that you exist in His living universe. You will learn to love the earth that offers you everything, the

115

water which you drink and that is life, the air that you breathe, the sun that gives you heat, and the children and elderly who discover the truth on their long journeys."

Amaru was shining. His light enveloped me. My feelings were indescribable. He looked at me very seriously and then continued speaking.

"If you deny this possibility, you will lose your natural brilliance. Learn to listen to yourself and to the one who calls you. Make sure that love is always present in your glance. Happily, the times are changing. Now, everyone can express their thoughts without any danger—other than their own mistakes. They are not punished, incarcerated, or killed for speaking out as has been the custom throughout history. The struggle will be more internal and personal. Intellectuals and mystics are coming close to each other. Scientists…"

"In the field of physics perhaps?" I mused.

"…and those who study the human brain or psychiatrists are the mystics of this epoch. They may only confirm what we already know—that we are fundamentally spiritual beings. We knew it for thousands of years but then we forgot it."

"These mystics are different," I thought.

"A mystic is not a saintly person," he explained "He does not costume himself in priestly habits or in the uniforms of other groups. Throughout the world, cultists wear peculiar colors, worship pictures, or imitate Jesus Christ's appearance. The mystic develops within himself a true and swift contact with divinity in its different manifestations. He understands the divine principles and the cosmic forces of Nature."

"The mystic sees Inti as the Great Intelligence within himself and everywhere. He knows that—anytime and anywhere—he can direct himself to Inti within. He does not need a special place like a church to pray. We always find Inti in our inner temple. He listens to us.

"Well, let's go and have dinner before Mamá bothers calling for us," he said while standing up.

I had not realized how the time had raced by during these days. It seemed a very short time to me. We walked slowly

116

on the way to my parents' home. We found my mother at the door.

"I was about to go and look for you. You should remember the hours of the meals every day or they will not appear," she said smiling.

"Why should mealtimes be fixed?" I wondered.

"It is better. It is a sort of discipline," he answered.

He put his right arm on my right shoulder almost embracing me. We entered the porch together and sat down for the last dinner with Amaru.

In the country, we go to bed early. We rest when the sun also 'goes to sleep', and we rise with it. One can gain quite a lot by getting out of bed early—at the very least one can enjoy nature. Like a child, it slowly arouses from sleep with the sun. Life is reborn in each dawn with much peace and love. It is too bad that—instead of enjoying creation and being happy—mankind lives each day pressured by tension and destroying nature.

Father said, "The pressures of life are so great that man in his pride cannot, or does not want to, recognize the stupidity of his acts. He has to do this in order to change and live happily."

Amaru added, "But now people from all social classes are actively searching to comprehend their lives and the reason for their existence."

"Of course," Father agreed. "There are beings (only a few) who are searching for an answer to their questions that neither politicians, scientists, nor the church can give them. These people are realizing that science and religion—instead of uniting them—drive them further apart. That is what comes from the thoughts of the divisive man. It separates us from the reality of physical life of today. Some people understand that modern science and religion cannot accept or conceive the integrated, complete totality. Many of these few take the highest interest in the esoteric teachings of

117

past generations. These are the only authentic teachings, anyway."

"Even though they are a little difficult to understand by the illustrations and terms that they use," Amaru said smiling.

"Correct," replied my father. "Even fewer people relate this knowledge to the daily materialistic life that we live. We ought to put this into practice daily."

I said, "Also, other sincerely concerned people turn to foreign spiritual traditions. They hope to find answers to their unknowns—answers that they were not able to find in their own religions."

"But those are foreign cultures," Father said. "Besides which, we have already lived and experimented in former reincarnations. It is a waste of time now. For some reason we are born and we live here. That is the ground for what we do. Besides, foreign spiritual traditions have completely different evolutionary schemes. People feel attracted to cults or to teachers who seem to answer the requirements of mankind. They like the new doctrine of creation and evolution. As we know, these are two events that happened one after the other. They do not contradict one another."

Amaru said, "Any secondhand knowledge is dangerous. People believe in something easily, but they do not live or practice that belief so easily. They like to listen but not to obey. Knowledge can be very good, but if man doesn't make it his own—doesn't accept it and live it—the knowledge is not more than a mental exercise that will deceive him."

"It is illusory, " I agreed.

Father added, "The Occidental countries put a great deal of value on intellect. Then man proclaims himself a god— he believes himself to be owner and possessor of all that exists. Fortunately, a universal consciousness is being born. People are gathering to join similar ideals, and this is good. Like attracts like. With respect to their differences, I believe that they now share the same universal message."

Amaru said, "Antonio[14] explained that to be born and to die are of equal significance." He gave me a pointed look. "I

118

touch this theme again because death frightens you, and soon you are going to face it. [15] Death should worry you no more than going to sleep every night and waking up in the morning. Sleeping is death and waking is rebirth. Each day is a life—so simple without more significance. The man who is not spiritual or hasn't even truly understood his origin is afraid of death. Also this fear comes from the way in which he conducts his life."

"Death is a journey between one existence and the other," my father said. "If one believes that death is an eternal ending, the values of his life will necessarily be different. Nothing will convince him to the contrary because he does not see otherwise. He denies and will not recognize the truth. It is necessary to understand that death is a transition. It is like going on vacation to rest and analyze what we learned after the school days during various months of the year. Then we return to classes to continue learning new lessons or to repeat them if necessary. For now, there is no way to convince anybody that there is life after death. You can only feel it for yourself or have the masters show it to you. Besides it does not make sense to waste time in such discussion."

"I believe that birth and death are two beautiful experiences for growing," I said.

Amaru said, "In childbirth, the mother has an initiation because she brings in a new life. This initiation will be clear—even though she may not be aware of it—depending on the love that she felt when she conceived. A mother usually isn't cognizant of this initiation; she simply feels an indescribable happiness. The baby's new little body brings energy, spirit, that it constructed and occupied. Birth is the materialization of the being. However, one must not think that all women must bear children to feel fulfillment. This is an error. Having children is not the only function of women. Fundamentally women are the balance to man. This is the true reason for men and woman to be here. They are equal. It is the female wisdom that balances the power

119

of the male. Both are sparks of creation—completely equal, though opposites."

"Undoubtedly, the birth of a child is a special and happy event. What about afflicted children—for example a child with Down's syndrome—what happens?" I asked.

Amaru declared, "Children with Down's syndrome are not deformed. Perhaps medicine views them as such because it does not see in the *beyond*.

"Humans with Down's syndrome are the first earthly incarnation of a spirit-Inti who is evolving from a denser planet—of a lower evolutionary vibration than our earth. These people have learned the lessons of that planet. Now they take their second phase on earth. As they still don't know differently, they construct these bodies that are familiar regarding their former experience. Is this clear?"

"Extremely clear," I said, enthused.

Amaru continued, "All that exists has a destiny, a life, a purpose for existence—individually making good use of its freedom. It is important that we have the opportunity to improve life with each return."

He made a spiral with his hand. "We ascend, we never descend, there is no involution. A being can be stuck but never descends."

"Are you saying that life is always an ascending spiral?" I asked.

"Correct," Amaru answered, smiling. "You always clarify my ideas with your words. How good."

"No, Master. Your expressions are always very clear," I replied. "I only want to be sure that I understand."

"Once sure, you must carry it into practice," Amaru said. "This means that you should tell people what you know; you have to affirm what you know. You don't have to explain how or why you know it, much less enter into a discussion. That is all. Your actions will always demonstrate what you are saying."

"An action is worth a thousand words," my father agreed. "Men will remember you by your actions—not by your words. However, it is necessary to know when to teach."

"You can teach only those who want to learn," Amaru said. "It is not good to speak to people who do not want to listen to you. Those who do will come voluntarily and will question you. I have told you before—wait, do not rush."

"Be certain that they do not think that you are talking about a religion," my father said. "Religions are not eternal nor will they ever be; they were created by men, not by Inti. You will be speaking of another path, a path that is within each person.

"Man does not belong to earth. He is a cosmic being. In his evolution he takes different steps—as Amaru was saying. Every spirit that incarnates on a planet constructs his body according to the laws of the nature, unless it is the first time. In such a case, he will build his body according to what he knew on his former home planet.

"That other road of which you will speak will produce a revolution. If someone were to realize who he is, he would go into shock. The realization would traumatize his life."

Smiling, Amaru said, "Catastrophes happen to everyone. These bring back memory of the past or block memory. So it occurred with our past. There are parts that we have wholly forgotten. We are oblivious to large sections of history, thanks to cataclysms that happened from time to time. People have perished by the thousands in each one of these events; new people are born and begin another time.

"Now it is late. I am going to take my leave because I will be leaving very early tomorrow—at dawn."

He surprised us! What a grim moment! For an instant I forgot that the Master had to go and that his illustrious and invaluable visit had ended. Father hugged him firmly and cried. Perhaps because he knew that Amaru would not be seen anymore on this earth. Amaru maintained his serenity. Mother cried with my father as she hugged Amaru with much love.

Amaru regarded her tenderly—I believe also sadly. Then, he hugged my mother and said:, "Mamay, I love you very much.

Thank you for all that you gave me these days—your love and your rich food. Soon, we will see each other on the other side."

My mother did not seem to grasp his last words, or she did not hear them.

"You do not have to thank me for anything. It is you whom we have to thank. Greetings to all of your family. I have prepared a little something for you for the road." Hugging him again, she handed him a small cloth bag.

"Don't stop being a mother," Amaru said to her and gave her a kiss.

I did not know what to do. Like my father I had a lump in my throat that would not let me breathe, much less speak.

"You don't have to say anything," Amaru faltered. He seemed caught up in the emotional moment and looked at me with extreme love.

I hugged him firmly and was scarcely able to talk. "Thank you, dear Master. Many thanks."

"You are my family, too," he said and went to bed.

The three of us remained silent for a good while.

Finally my father—making an effort to breathe deeply—said, "Tomorrow is a new day. We have to return to Cuzco."

"To *Quosqo*, dear father—to *Quosqo*," I said. My jest served its purpose; they both smiled. We were gradually finding our composure.

When the mood lifted, I asked, "Papá, how old will Amaru be?"

"There is no old age nor youth in the Wise One," he answered me. "He is a timeless Ancient One."

"I understand what you want to say, but…"

"I wish that young people had the wisdom of the elderly," he interrupted. "Then they wouldn't commit blunders in life, which then cause sorrow. Amaru is an Ancient Wise One with the optimism of youth. He has the steadfastness and wisdom of a venerable elder without being one."

I believed that said everything. I hugged Father, kissed both of them, and went to bed.

I lay on my bed for a moment. I closed my eyes and began to *see* extremely beautiful scenes from my past. I visited Vil-

122

lage A. I saw Amaru Yupanqui Puma—Nina Soncco—again. No time had elapsed. In that dimension there was no time. I felt the urgent need to speak—as though someone within me needed expression.

I said, "I am remembering all that I have seen, heard, and what will be.

"I remember the titanic Wise Ones whom I knew, those Andeans who are the origin of man."

My mother excarnated the following year.

Meanwhile, I finished writing this book.

Master Amaru Cusiyupanqui and the Sacred Lake had allowed me to experience the events in this book. Other adventures happened during that time, about which I will write soon.

Epilogue

Res Non Verba
Samana Wasi Is Now a Reality

Someone said, "The most insignificant of actions is worth more than the greatest of intentions." This proverb lives in the contents of this book. It is true that the idea matured when the intention appeared, but it did result in action.

Without mentioning the time it took to form a staff of helpers, Samana Wasi was born as a family on the winter solstice of 1989. Thus began the solidification of an objective of the foundation that Antón Ponce de León and his wife Regia Astete had incubated. It is worthwhile reiterating the goals of the foundation.

I. SOCIAL SERVICE
A. A boarding school for destitute children under seven years old. This provides them with a home in the true sense of the word until they become adults.
B. Board and care facility for the destitute elderly. This provides them with lodging, food, clothing, and health care.

II. RESEARCH
A. Of the cosmogenic and cosmological Quechua past.
B. In the Schools of Life.
C. Alternate medical systems.
D. New techniques of agriculture and cattle farming.

III. PERSONAL DEVELOPMENT
A. For those who search for spiritual growth.
B. The family continues to grow. Soon there will be thirty young children who will acquire the tools they need to seek their happiness.
C. Samana Wasi practices the four conditions that Albert Camus proposed in order to reach happiness.
    1. TO LIVE IN OPEN AIR—The healthful atmosphere

of the Urubamba valley has no equal.

2. TO BE LOVED—This is truly a family united by love and for love.

3. TO BE FREE OF ALL AMBITION—The only ambition is to share more happiness with as many people as possible.

4. CREATIVITY—As well as classroom instruction, Samana Wasi has its own library. There are workshops for art, crafts, and responsibilities—similar to other educational and recreational facilities—to inspire creative freedom. The results are surprising.

Our purpose is to give an authentic integrated training to each person—an education for life. Each child lives surrounded by love, friendship, honor, justice, and—above all—fraternity.

Another philosopher said, "We love and admire the antique, but we forget the beauty of the ancient ones." Samana Wasi is doing its part. Very soon it will welcome the first little *Wise Ones* of either gender. The infrastructure is prepared.

An inevitable question is: How solvent is this benevolent work? Faith moves mountains. Its founder is a man of faith. However, faith is never passive. It is necessary to go at least halfway to receive provision. The means that God has provided until now are the royalties from Antón's books and the honoraria and donations received through his lectures. Other important sources are the direct collaboration of generous people and Caritas of Cuzco. Any contribution will be welcome and put to good use. We are working with strict observance of propriety. Please direct all correspondence to:

Antón Ponce de León Paiva
Casilla de Correo No. 575
Cuzco, Peru, South America
FAX +51-84-233233

Thank you! May that which has been sown reach harvest!

Mario Cutimbo Hinojosa

Endnotes

Prologue

[1] The Illac Uma master has since passed away. He was a descendant of the Runasimi, and was the inheritor of the Quechua tradition and cosmogony. The name Nina Soncco means *Heart of Fire*.

[2] To protect privacy, this is what I shall call that beautiful place I visited for seven unforgettable days—though you may not believe this, my dear brother and sister—days that marked my life for the future with fire.

[3] See Ponce's first book in this series, *The Wisdom of the Ancient One*.

[4] The House of Rest.

The First Day

[1] He was my master, the successor of Nina Soncco, the living Illac Uma, and the possessor of Truth that I knew, as well as much more truth that I did not know.

[2] Nina Soncco had also told me this.

[3] Amaru surely meant eons and many reincarnations.

[4] Lucas was the son of Yupanqui Puma.

[5] I call them the blue jeans generation.

[6] Perhaps the noise hides their confusion.

[7] He should have said, "Few *of us* remain." However, his humility prevented this.

[8] It did happen that way. Unprepared, I had to renounce many things and endured much stress. I sacrificed for the sake of my dearly loved ones. It was very difficult, but I did it. I had to make difficult decisions. Afterwards I realized that I had not renounced a thing. How deluded we are as we walk through this earthly life! Finally we remove our blindfolds. Then our constraints disappear and we can clearly perceive the path that roused us to examine the times.

[9] See *The Wisdom of the Ancient One*.

[10] Koriwairachina is the mountain base of Chupani where "the wind is filled with gold."

[11] My father also walked in silence when traveling by foot.

[12] *The Water of Life,* by John W. Armstrong. "Ein ganz besonderer Saft. Urin" by Carmen Phomes.

The Second Day

[1] Urpi means dove.

[2] The *Place of the Spirits* has been known by these names for centuries.

[3] Construction has already begun on this building.

The Third Day

[1] Tantanmarka is a mountain located northeast of Samana Wasi.

[2] The 'official' dialect of Spanish.

[3] An instrument used to call an assembly to attention.

The Fourth Day

1. The Runasimi named it the City of Light, the Place of Light, and the Land of Light.

2. Experts believe that they have a monopoly on the Great Knowledge. That is to say, they are the theorists of spirituality—the armchair spiritualists. They certainly do need to know that spirituality is lived and practiced, but not discussed. It is carried through; it is served. We have seen time and again that there is no spiritual growth without service.

3. Our kitchen was a mud hearth fueled with firewood.

4. Besides, this is a metaphysical obligation.

5. Amaru refers to establishing outer retreats as satellites to Village A.

6. House of the Sun or House of the Father.

7. As mentioned earlier, The House of Rest.

8. My father was a schoolteacher.

9. Bird fertilizer.

10. Temple of the Sun. It is the heart of Cuzco. *Korikancha* sounds better and is more authentic in Quechua.

11. The rainbow symbolizes union with Inti and peace.

12. The Sacred City of pre-historical origin that lies within the modern city of Cuzco.

13. Sometimes Amaru used the word 'pray' to also include the act of meditation.

14. Amaru's father.

15. I did not understand what he meant until later.

The First Book by
Antón Ponce de León Paiva
The Wisdom of the Ancient One

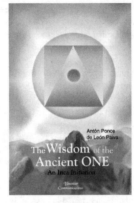

Trade Paper, 121 pages
$9.95
ISBN 1-885394-09-8

In her book, *It's All in The Playing*, Shirley MacLaine introduces us to Antón Ponce de León Paiva as a researcher for the UFO phenomenon; but in his book *The Wisdom of the Ancient ONE* he presents himself as the promising writer that he is.

The author tells the story of his initiation into an ancient Inca tradition. It is the first book to document this tradition of ancient Inca knowledge, a tradition still alive in the hidden regions of the Andes today.

What makes the story even more fascinating is the author's description of how he and his wife have used this ancient wisdom to guide them build a home for Peruvian orphans, a home where these children can live joyful and protected lives.

The seven days of initiation and the practical aspects of the structure of "Samana Wasi," the author's center, are described.

The book provides the reader with a deep understanding of Inca spirituality, as well as presenting an approach by which this understanding can be incorporated into one's daily life.

This is the story of an Inca initiation and how this ancient wisdom can be used in the world of the Twentieth Century.